TWELVE ANGRY MEN

REGINALD ROSE (1920–2002) was born and grew up in New York City. After Pearl Harbor he enlisted, and served in the Philippines and Japan as a First Lieutenant until 1946. Writing since he was a teenager, he sold the first of his many television plays, *The Bus to Nowhere*, in 1950. He was called for jury duty for the first time in 1954. It was a manslaughter case and the jury argued bitterly for eight hours before bringing in a unanimous verdict. He decided this was a powerful situation on which to base a television play, and wrote *Twelve Angry Men* as a live one-hour drama for CBS's *Studio One*. Its impact led to the film version in 1957, and he received Oscar nominations for Best Screenplay and Best Picture (as coproducer). The stage version was first produced in 1964, and revised versions in 1996 and 2004. In 1997 it was filmed for Showtime.

Other TV plays include *The Remarkable Incident at Carson Corners*, *Thunder on Sycamore Street*, *The Cruel Day*, *A Quiet Game of Cards*, *The Sacco-Vanzetti Story*, *Black Monday*, *Dear Friends*, *Studs Lonigan*, *The Rules of Marriage*, and the award-winning *Escape from Sobibor*. Rose created, supervised, and wrote many of the episodes of the TV series *The Defenders* (1961–1965). His films include *Crime in the Streets*, *Dino*, *Man of the West*, *The Man in the Net*, *Baxter!*, *Somebody Killed Her Husband*, *The Wild Geese; The Sea Wolves*, and the film version of *Whose Life Is It Anyway?* He published *Six Television Plays*; *The Thomas Book*, written for children; and a memoir, *Undelivered Mail*.

Nominated six times, he won Emmys in 1954, 1962, and 1963. Among his many awards are the Berlin Golden Bear (1957); Writers Guild of America awards, including the Lifetime Achievement Award; and three Mystery Writers of America awards.

DAVID MAMET is the author of the plays *Oleanna*, *Glengarry Glen Ross* (1984 Pulitzer Prize and the New York Drama Critics Circle Award), *American Buffalo*, *A Life in the Theatre*, *Speed-the-Plow*, *Edmond*, *Lakeboat*, *The Water Engine*, *The Woods*, *Sexual Perversity in Chicago*, *Reunion*, *The Cryptogram* (1995

Obie Award), *The Old Neighborhood*, *Boston Marriage*, *Dr. Faustus*, and *Romance*. His translation and adaptations include *Red River* by Pierre Laville and *The Cherry Orchard*, *Three Sisters*, and *Uncle Vanya* by Anton Chekhov. His films include, as writer, *The Postman Always Rings Twice*, *The Verdict*, *The Untouchables*, *Hoffa*, *The Edge*, *Wag the Dog*, and *The Winslow Boy*; as writer/director, *House of Games*, *Oleanna*, *Homicide*, *The Spanish Prisoner*, *State and Main*, *Heist*, and *Spartan*. He is also the author of *Warm and Cold* and *Bar Mitzvah*, books for children with illustrations by Donald Sultan, and three other children's books: *Passover*, *The Duck and the Goat*, and *Henrietta*; five volumes of essays: *Writing in Restaurants*, *Some Freaks*, *The Cabin*, *Make-Believe Town*, and *Jaffsie and John Henry*; two books of poems: *The Hero Pony* and *Chinaman*; *Three Children's Plays*, *On Directing Film*, *True and False*, *Three Uses of the Knife: On the Nature and Purpose of Drama*, and the novels *The Village*, *The Old Religion*, and *Wilson*. Currently, he is cocreator of and executive producer for the CBS television series *The Unit*, for which he also writes and directs.

REGINALD ROSE

Twelve Angry Men

Introduction by DAVID MAMET

PENGUIN BOOKS

PENGUIN BOOKS
Published by the Penguin Group
Penguin Group (USA) Inc., 375 Hudson Street, New York, New York 10014, U.S.A.
Penguin Group (Canada), 90 Eglinton Avenue East, Suite 700, Toronto, Ontario,
Canada M4P 2Y3 (a division of Pearson Penguin Canada Inc.)
Penguin Books Ltd, 80 Strand, London WC2R 0RL, England
Penguin Ireland, 25 St Stephen's Green, Dublin 2, Ireland (a division of Penguin Books Ltd)
Penguin Group (Australia), 250 Camberwell Road, Camberwell, Victoria 3124,
Australia (a division of Pearson Australia Group Pty Ltd)
Penguin Books India Pvt Ltd, 11 Community Centre, Panchsheel Park,
New Delhi – 110 017, India
Penguin Group (NZ), 67 Apollo Drive, Rosedale, North Shore 0632,
New Zealand (a division of Pearson New Zealand Ltd)
Penguin Books (South Africa) (Pty) Ltd, 24 Sturdee Avenue, Rosebank,
Johannesburg 2196, South Africa

Penguin Books Ltd, Registered Offices: 80 Strand, London WC2R 0RL, England

First published in the United States of America by Dramatic Publishing Co. 1955
This edition with an introduction by David Mamet published in Penguin Books 2006

30 29 28 27 26 25 24

LIBRARY OF CONGRESS CATALOGING IN PUBLICATION DATA
Rose, Reginald.
Twelve angry men / Reginald Rose ; introduced by David Mamet.
p. cm. — (Penguin classics)
ISBN 978-0-14-310440-7
1. Legal drama, American.   I. Title.   II. Title: 12 angry men.   III. Series.
PS3535.O666T9 2006
812'.54—dc22   2006046006

Printed in the United States of America
Set in Sabon

Contents

Introduction

Our greatest American Philosopher, to my mind, was Eric Hoffer.

He was an immigrant kid. He never spent a day in school. He roamed the country during the Depression as a hobo and migrant worker. He wrote that some fellow from the Works Progress Administration rode into his hobo camp sometime in the thick of the Depression and said: "Who wants to work?" The volunteers were put on a flatbed truck and hauled some miles up into the mountains in California.

The WPA boss gave one man a compass and a map and said: "Build a road. Your road is to start *here*, and in three months I will meet you over *there*. Here are the specs. Take the tools off the truck and get to work."

Hoffer wrote that that is just what they did. There was enough talent and know-how on the truck, he wrote, to've built not only that road, but to have built America. For that, he said, was quite exactly how America was built—a group of reasonably intelligent workers took a simple plan, formed an ad-hoc group, and used their common sense and group spirit to execute it well.

There are, I think, two Americas. There is that which we decry on reading the newspapers. "Those fools," we say, of the group not of our political bent, "how in the *world* can they believe the nonsense they are spouting? How can intelligent people act that way?" This is the America of "them."

And then there is the America we participate in—that fairly friendly and reasonable group of diverse interests and talents, happy to pitch in, the America of "us." We see and participate in this group at the Little League, the Rotary, the Shul or Church, the block party, the sports bar—we speak its language in the conversation we strike up with the stranger in the airline departure lounge, in the chat with the other parents on the way to school, in the office jokes we share. This nonabstract, this real America, is a rather pleasant place. When we are not being actively divided—by religion or politics—we rest here in the default position of unity. Over time, we see, the reasonable often find a way to unite the seemingly irreconcilable claims of passion.

This process is the essence of our system of jurisprudence. The jury trial enshrines our belief in and our experience that the multitude of the wise is the treasure of the land. Most people, I believe, initially shun jury duty. The summons always seems to come at the least opportune time, and one might go kicking and screaming.

Once empanelled on the jury, however, one is subsumed by what one realizes is the essential component of American Democracy. On election day we vote, inwardly or openly maligning the other half of our society, those idiots who will not see the light. In the jury room we are humbled by the realization that there is no one home but us.

Here there are no hucksters, spending hundreds of millions on advertising, no stick figures throwing their jackets over their shoulder and grinning at the camera just like normal folks, no ginned-up controversies to enflame us against our neighbors.

In the courtroom we see a poor man or woman—perhaps a criminal, perhaps a victim—caught in the awesome engine of the State, and we are told that, for the period of our service, we *are* the State.

The lawyers can and will lie, elaborate, attempt to distract, embellish, and confuse; and nothing stands between the person in the box and the horror of an unchecked government except twelve diverse, reasonably intelligent people.

The jurors have been wrenched from their daily lives, and made to swear a terrible oath. This oath is of such strength that it makes that taken in the marriage ceremony seem—as indeed it may, sadly, generally prove—conditional.

The Bible abounds with adjurations against perjury. A vast amount of the Book of Proverbs deals with the Lord's horror of false witness. "Partiality in judging is not good. He who says to the wicked 'you are innocent' will be cursed and abhorred." "Witness not against your neighbor without cause," "A false witness will not go unpunished," "Do not favor the rich in judgment neither give preference to the poor."

Sitting in the jury box we console ourselves for the loss of time and income, thinking, "Before God, that could be me on trial. If that were so, God forbid, I would want those in the jury to be as responsible as I pledge to be and as terrified of error as I am."

The jury is that same group of individuals who can, through divisive words, be congealed into a mob; who can, through persuasion or art, form itself into an audience. The audience suspends its disbelief in order to receive entertainment. As, curiously, does the mob—which is merely an audience enflamed, and moved by its righteous wrath, to crime. But the jury sets aside its prejudices, to aspire to the highest state of humanity: the capacity to use reason to overcome animal passion.

They are instructed to apply the standard of "reasonable doubt." Each member will, of course, interpret this finally indefinable notion in his or her own way; and this is the genius of the jury trial, that these idiosyncratic understandings and applications of this abstract notion must each be defended to the group. The untutored, diverse group must then apply its own communal understanding of an abstract concept to a set of debatable facts and conflicting presentations, and arrive at a unanimous conclusion.

Here the mega-state, outrageous in its multiplicity, absurd in the distance between manufacturer and end-user, between politician and voter, between entertainer and audience, is reduced to the size of a primitive clan.

The drama this clan acts out is immemorial. The clan asks: "What shall we do with X?" And the elders reply: "Hold him here, while we retire and deliberate."

The protagonist of a drama is caught in circumstances not of his own making.

The hero of a tragedy discovers, at the play's dénouement, that the affective circumstances he thought external to himself were actually brought into being by flaws in his own character.

Tragedy is the more difficult form to write, as it is a closed system. The tragedy must resolve (both for the hero and for the viewer) in revelation that the answer was before them all the time. This revelation, then, must be both surprising and inevitable. Any attempt by the author to mitigate the inevitable closed progression toward knowledge will weaken the tragedy. (The writer of the tragedy can not bring in conflicts and resolutions not brought into being by the hero's character defects. He cannot advance the plot by whim.)

The writer of the drama, on the other hand, has a wide license. He or she may introduce, at will, external circumstances to beat the band: the hero may be assigned a physical illness, a rotten set of parents, the antagonist of an evil government or employer, or a socially precarious status. As these states are not of the hero's own device (they are merely assigned), the tools to be used in their vanquishment may be more or less arbitrary.

Similarly, the very *setting* of the drama may be used for convenient effect. (Set *Hamlet* in a castle, a pawnshop, or a submarine, it's the same play. The setting has no dramatic weight.)

Writers of the drama, on the other hand, may, to provide a catalyst, moor or abandon their protagonists in that space the very egress from which provides dramatic fodder. (The proverbial example being the group of snowbound travelers stuck in the inn or its equivalent, e.g., *Bus Stop*, *The Petrified Forest*, *Dead End*, *Truckline Café*, *The Waters of the Moon*, and, to stretch a point, *The Cherry Orchard*.)

These plays are all, generically, "gang dramas."

That is, *formally*, they do not differ from their (generally coeval) counterparts on the comedy side, the films of the Marx Brothers. In the gang drama the protagonist or hero is split into many parts, each part (or character) standing for a different aspect of the hero's consciousness.

These warring factions (as the opposed factions of the consciousness in the individual) must work from their initial irreconcilable positions, to find unity where none could have been suspected. (They may be aided in the struggle if "snowbound at an inn," as they have conveniently been provided with "no way out.") At the end of the gang drama, the individuals (the play and, thus, the audience) have seen unity established and, so, are made more whole.

In the bad version of this gang drama the audience is given the gift of a predictable ending: "Black people are people, too," "Gay people are people, too," "HIV-positive people are people, too." This foreseeable, universally accepted message is a sop to the self-esteem of the audience, which has been deprived of the experience of revelation. Self-congratulation sends the audience out into the night in a state of euphoria that will not last past the end of the block. But the good drama (e.g., *Twelve Angry Men*) leaves the issue in doubt. It enmeshes the audience in the problems of the protagonists so that they may consider the arguments, now one, now the other, until, when hope is gone, persistence (of the author and of his or her creations) brings revelation, and the audience may leave the play surprised by the discovery of the possibility of peace.

Twelve Angry Men

Cast

Twelve Angry Men was produced on Broadway by The Roundabout Theatre Company: Todd Haimes, Ellen Richard, and Julia Levy. It opened at the American Airlines Theatre on October 28, 2004, with the following cast:

JUROR ONE	Mark Blum
JUROR TWO	Kevin Geer
JUROR THREE	Philip Bosco
JUROR FOUR	James Rebhorn
JUROR FIVE	Michael Mastro
JUROR SIX	Robert Clohessy
JUROR SEVEN	John Pankow
JUROR EIGHT	Boyd Gaines
JUROR NINE	Tom Aldredge
JUROR TEN	Peter Friedman
JUROR ELEVEN	Larry Bryggman
JUROR TWELVE	Adam Trese
GUARD	Matte Osian
JUDGE'S VOICE	Robert Prosky

Directed by Scott Ellis
Set designed by Allen Moyer
Costumes designed by Michael Krass
Lighting desing by Paul Palazzo

Sound design by Brian Ronan
Original compositions by John Gromada

Production Stage Manager	Roy Harris
Stage Manager	Leslie C. Lyter
Assistant Director	Gwynn MacDonald

Characters

Setting—The jury room of a New York Court of Law
Time—1957

ACT I

The jury room of a New York Court of Law, 1957. A very hot summer afternoon.

It is a large, drab, bare room in need of painting, with three windows in the back wall through which can be seen the New York skyline. Off the jury room is a washroom with wash-basin, soap, and towels (visible on stage) and a lavatory beyond. A large, scarred table is center with twelve chairs around it. A bench stands against the wall and there are several extra chairs and a small table in the room, plus a watercooler, with paper cups and a wastebasket and an electric fan over the bench and a clock above the cooler and row of hooks for coats, with a shelf over it. There are pencils, pads, and ashtrays on the table. At night the room is lit by fluorescent lighting with the switch next to the door.

When the CURTAIN *rises, the room is empty. The voice of the* JUDGE *is heard.*

JUDGE'S VOICE . . . and that concludes the court's explanation of the legal aspects of this case. And now, gentlemen of the jury, I come to my final instruction to you. Murder in the first degree—premeditated homicide—is the most serious charge tried in our criminal courts. You've listened to the testimony and you've had the law read to you and interpreted as it applies to this case. It now becomes your duty to try and separate the facts from the fancy. One man is dead. The life of another is at stake. I urge you to deliberate honestly and thoughtfully. If there is a reasonable doubt—then you must bring me a verdict of "not guilty." If, however, there is no reasonable doubt—then you must, in good conscience, find the accused guilty. However you decide, your verdict must be unanimous. In the event you find the accused guilty, the bench will not entertain a recommendation for mercy. The death sentence is mandatory in this case.

The door opens and the GUARD *enters. He carries a clipboard with a list of the jurors.*

I don't envy you your job. You are faced with a grave responsibility. Thank you, gentlemen.

There is a brief pause. Sound of JURORS *walking, talking.*

GUARD: All right, let's move along, gentlemen.

The JURORS *enter.*

The GUARD *checks his list.*

The 9TH JUROR, *an old man, crosses, goes into the washroom, and exits to the lavatory.*

The 4TH JUROR *begins to read a newspaper. Several* JURORS *open the windows. Others move awkwardly about the room. There is no conversation for a few moments. The* 3RD JUROR *takes out some notes and studies them. The* 2ND JUROR *crosses to the watercooler, and gets a cup of water. The* FOREMAN *tears a sheet from a notepad and tears up little slips of paper for ballots. The* GUARD *crosses to the* 12TH JUROR *and checks his name. The* 7TH JUROR *crosses to the* 4TH JUROR *and offers him a stick of gum. The* 4TH JUROR *shakes his head.*

7TH JUROR [*turning to the* 8TH JUROR]: Do you want some gum?

8TH JUROR [*smiling*]: No, thanks.

The 7TH JUROR *vigorously chews a piece of gum himself and crosses to the* 6TH JUROR.

7TH JUROR [*mopping his brow*]: Y'know something? I phoned up for the weather. This is the hottest day of the year.

The 6TH JUROR *nods and gazes out of the window.*

You'd think they'd at least air-condition the place. I almost dropped dead in court.

GUARD: OK, gentlemen. Everybody's here. If there's anything you want, I'm right outside. Just knock.

The Guard exits and in the silence the sound is heard of the door being locked.

5TH JUROR: I never knew they locked the door.

10TH JUROR: Sure they lock the door. What'd you think?

5TH JUROR: I don't know. It just never occurred to me.

The 10TH JUROR *crosses and pauses beside the* FOREMAN *and indicates the slips of paper.*

10TH JUROR: Hey, what's that for?

FOREMAN: Well, I figured we might want to vote by ballots.

10TH JUROR: Great idea! Maybe we can get him elected senator. [*He laughs until he begins to cough.*]

The FOREMAN *looks at his watch and compares it with the clock. The* 3RD JUROR *takes a cup of water from the watercooler, moves to the* 2ND JUROR, *and looks around the room as he sips the water.*

3RD JUROR [*to the* 2ND JUROR]: How'd you like it?

2ND JUROR [*mildly*]: I don't know, it was pretty interesting.

3RD JUROR: Yeah? I was falling asleep.

2ND JUROR: I mean, I've never been on a jury before.

3RD JUROR: Really? I've sat on juries, and it always amazes me the way these lawyers can talk, and talk and talk, even when the case is as obvious as this one. I mean, did you ever hear so much talk about nothing?

2ND JUROR: Well, I guess they're entitled.

3RD JUROR: Sure they are. Everybody deserves a fair trial. That's the system. Listen, I'm the last one to say anything against it, but I'm telling you sometimes I think we'd be better off if we took these tough kids and slapped 'em down before they make trouble, you know? Save us a lot of time and money.

The 2ND JUROR *looks nervously at the* 3RD JUROR, *nods, rises, moves to the watercooler, refills his cup and stands alone, sipping.*

7TH JUROR [*to the* FOREMAN]: Hey, how about getting started here?

3RD JUROR: Yeah, let's get this over with. We've probably all got things to do.

FOREMAN: Well, I was figuring we'd take a five-minute break. I mean, the old man's in the bathroom . . .

5TH JUROR [*to the* FOREMAN, *hesitantly*]: Are we going to sit in order?

FOREMAN: I don't know.

The 8TH JUROR *is looking out the window.*

12TH JUROR [*to the* 8TH JUROR]: Not a bad view.

The 8TH JUROR *nods.*

What d'you think of the case?

The 8TH JUROR *doesn't answer.*

It had a lot of interest for me. No dead spots—know what I mean? I'll tell you we were lucky to get a murder case. I figured us for a burglary or an assault or something. Those can be the dullest. [*He looks out of the window.*] Say, isn't that the Woolworth building?

8TH JUROR: That's right.

12TH JUROR: Funny, I've lived here all my life and I've never been in it.

The 8TH JUROR *gazes out of the window. The* 12TH JUROR *looks at him for a moment then moves away.*

7TH JUROR [*to the* 10TH JUROR]: Goddamn waste of time. [*He laughs.*]

10TH JUROR: Yeah, can you imagine, sitting there for three days just for this?

7TH JUROR: And what about that business with the knife? I mean, asking grown-up people to believe that kind of bullshit.

10TH JUROR: Well, look, you've gotta expect that. You know what you're dealing with.

7TH JUROR: Yeah, I suppose so.

The 10TH JUROR *blows his nose vigorously.*

What's the matter, you got a cold?

10TH JUROR: And how. These hot weather colds can kill you. I can hardly touch my nose. Know what I mean? [*He blows his nose loudly.*]

7TH JUROR: Well, your horn's all right. Now try your lights. [*He climbs on to the bench and tries the fan.*] Oh, that's beautiful, the fan doesn't work. [*He steps down.*] Somebody take a letter to the mayor. "Dear Stingy . . ."

FOREMAN [*about the fan*]: Let me take a look at it.

The 3RD JUROR *moves above the* 4TH JUROR, *leans over and scans the* 4TH JUROR's *newspaper. The* FOREMAN *climbs on the bench and examines the fan.*

It doesn't work. [*He climbs down.*]

3RD JUROR [*to the* 4TH JUROR]: I didn't get a chance to look at the newspapers today. Anything new going on?

4TH JUROR: I was just wondering how the market closed.

3RD JUROR: I wouldn't know. Say, are you on the Exchange or something?

4TH JUROR: I'm a broker.

3RD JUROR: Really? I run a messenger service. "The Beck and Call Company." The name's my wife's idea. I employ thirty-seven people. . . . Started with nothing.

7TH JUROR [*looking at his watch*]: Hey, Mr. Foreman, let's go. What d'you say?

FOREMAN: All right, gentlemen. Let's take seats.

7TH JUROR [*to the* 2ND JUROR]: This better be fast. I got tickets to a ball game tonight. Yankees—Cleveland. We got this new kid pitching, Modjelewski, or whatever his name is. He's a bull, this kid. [*He shoots his hand forward and out to indicate the path of a curve ball.*] Shhooooom. A real jug handle. *There is no reaction at all from the* 2ND JUROR.

You're quite a ball fan, aren't you? [*He turns to the* FOREMAN.] Where do you want us to sit?

FOREMAN: Well, I was thinking we ought to sit in order, by jury numbers. [*He points with each number.*] Two, three, four, and so on, if that's OK with you gentlemen?

10TH JUROR: What's the difference?

4TH JUROR: I think it's reasonable to sit according to number.

10TH JUROR [*rising*]: Let it be. [*He moves and sits on chair 10.*] *The* JURORS *begin to take their seats. The* 8TH JUROR *continues to stare out of the window. The* 9TH JUROR *is still in the lavatory.*

12TH JUROR [*to the* 11TH JUROR]: What was your impression of the prosecuting attorney?

11TH JUROR [*with a German accent*]: I beg pardon?

12TH JUROR: I thought he was really sharp. I mean, the way he hammered home his points, one by one, in logical sequence. It takes a good brain to do that. I was very impressed.

11TH JUROR: Yes, I think he did an expert job.

12TH JUROR: I mean, he had a lot of drive, too. Real drive.

7TH JUROR: OK, let's get this show on the road.

FOREMAN [*to the* 8TH JUROR]: How about sitting down?

The 8TH JUROR *does not hear the* FOREMAN.

The gentleman at the window.

The 8TH JUROR *turns, startled.*

How about sitting down?

8TH JUROR: Oh, I'm sorry. [*He moves to his chair and sits.*]

The 9TH JUROR *enters the washroom from the lavatory and washes his hands.*

10TH JUROR [*across the table to the* 4TH JUROR]: It's pretty tough to figure, isn't it? A kid kills his father. Bing! Just like that.

12TH JUROR: Well, if you analyze the figures . . .

10TH JUROR: What figures? It's those people! I'm tellin' you they let the kids run wild up there. Well, maybe it serves 'em right. Know what I mean?

The FOREMAN *crosses to the washroom door.*

7TH JUROR [*to the* 5TH JUROR]: Hey, you a Yankee fan?

5TH JUROR: No. Milwaukee.

7TH JUROR: Milwaukee! That's like being hit on the head with a crowbar once a day. Listen, who they got—I'm asking you, who they got besides great groundskeepers?

FOREMAN [*to the* 9TH JUROR]: We'd like to get started.

The 9TH JUROR *enters from the washroom.*

9TH JUROR: I'm sorry.

The 9TH JUROR *crosses and takes his seat.*

7TH JUROR: Milwaukee!

FOREMAN: All right. Now you gentlemen can handle this any way you want to. I mean, I'm not going to have any rules. If we want to discuss first and then vote, that's one way. Or we can vote right now to see how we stand. [*He pauses and looks around.*] Well, that's all I have to say.

4TH JUROR: I think it's customary to take a preliminary vote.

7TH JUROR: Yeah, let's vote. Who knows, maybe we can all go home.

FOREMAN: It's up to you. Just let's remember we've got a first degree murder charge here. If we vote "guilty," we send the accused to the electric chair. That's mandatory.

4TH JUROR: I think we all know that.

3RD JUROR: Come on, let's vote.

1OTH JUROR: Yeah, let's see who's where.

FOREMAN: Anybody doesn't want to vote? [*He looks around.*] *The others are silent.*

All right. This has to be a twelve-to-nothing vote either way. That's the law. OK, are we ready? All those voting "guilty" raise your hands.

Seven or eight hands go up immediately. Several others go up more slowly. Everyone looks around the table as the FORE-MAN *rises and begins to count hands. The* 9TH JUROR's *hand goes up now, and all hands are raised except the* 8TH JUROR's. . . . Nine—ten—eleven. That's eleven for "guilty." OK. "Not guilty"?

The 8TH JUROR *slowly raises his hand.*

One. Right. OK, eleven to one—"guilty." Now we know where we are. [*He resumes his seat.*]

1OTH JUROR: Boy-oh-boy! There's always one.

7TH JUROR [*after a pause*]: So, what do we do now?

8TH JUROR: Well, I guess we talk.

1OTH JUROR: Boy-oh-boy!

3RD JUROR [*leaning over toward the* 8TH JUROR]: Well, look, do you really think he's innocent?

8TH JUROR: I don't know.

3RD JUROR: I mean, let's be reasonable. You sat in court and heard the same things we did. The man's a dangerous killer. You could see it.

8TH JUROR: The man! He's sixteen years old.

3RD JUROR: Well, that's old enough. He knifed his own father. Four inches into the chest.

6TH JUROR [*to the* 8TH JUROR]: It's pretty obvious. I mean, I was convinced from the first day.

3RD JUROR: Well, who wasn't? [*To the* 8TH JUROR.] I really think this is one of those open and shut things. They proved it a dozen different ways. Would you like me to list them for you?

8TH JUROR: No.

1OTH JUROR: Then what do you want?

8TH JUROR: Nothing. I just want to talk.

7TH JUROR: Well, what's there to talk about? Eleven men here agree. Nobody had to think twice about it, except you.

1OTH JUROR: I want to ask you something. Do you believe his story?

8TH JUROR: I don't know whether I believe it or not. Maybe I don't.

7TH JUROR: So what'd you vote "not guilty" for?

8TH JUROR: There were eleven votes for "guilty." It's not easy for me to raise my hand and send a boy off to die without talking about it first.

7TH JUROR: Who says it's easy for me?

8TH JUROR: No one.

7TH JUROR: What, just because I voted fast? I think the guy's guilty. You couldn't change my mind if you talked for a hundred years.

8TH JUROR: I'm not trying to change your mind. It's just that we're talking about somebody's life here. I mean, we can't decide in five minutes. Suppose we're wrong?

7TH JUROR: Suppose we're wrong! Suppose this whole building fell on my head. You can suppose anything.

8TH JUROR: That's right.

7TH JUROR [after a pause]: What's the difference how long it takes? We honestly think he's guilty. So suppose we finish in five minutes? So what?

8TH JUROR: Let's take an hour. The ball game doesn't start till eight o'clock.

7TH JUROR [smiling]: OK, slugger, be my guest.

There is a silence.

FOREMAN [hesitantly]: Well, who's got something to say?

He looks at the 2ND JUROR.

How about you?

2ND JUROR: Not me.

9TH JUROR: I'm willing to put in an hour.

1OTH JUROR: Great. I heard a pretty good story last night. This woman comes running into the doctor's office, stripped to the waist—

8TH JUROR: That's not what we're sitting here for.

10TH JUROR: All right, then you tell me. What are we sitting here for?

8TH JUROR: Maybe for no reason. I don't know. Look, this boy's been kicked around all his life. You know—living in a slum, his mother dead since he was nine. He spent a year and a half in an orphanage while his father served a jail term for forgery. That's not a very good head start. He's had a pretty terrible sixteen years. I think maybe we owe him a few words. That's all.

10TH JUROR: I don't mind telling you this, mister. We don't owe him a thing. He got a fair trial, didn't he? What d'you think the trial cost? He's lucky he got it. Know what I mean? [*He rises and looks around at the others.*] Look, we're all grown-ups here. We heard the facts, didn't we? Now, you're not going to tell us that we're supposed to believe that kid, knowing what he is. Listen, I've lived among 'em all my life. You can't believe a word they say. I mean, they're born liars.

9TH JUROR: It suddenly occurs to me that you must be an ignorant man.

10TH JUROR: What do you mean? What's he talking about?

9TH JUROR: Do you think you have a monopoly on the truth?

10TH JUROR: What are you making a Federal Case out of it for? [*To the others.*] How d'ya like this guy?

9TH JUROR [*to the others*]: I think certain things should be pointed out to this man.

3RD JUROR: All right. It's not Sunday. We don't need a sermon in here.

10TH JUROR: Monopoly! For Chrissakes.

The 9TH JUROR *half rises but then feels the* 8TH JUROR's *hand firmly on his arm, gently pulling him down. The* 12TH JUROR *doodles on his notepad.*

4TH JUROR: If we're going to discuss this case, let's stick to the facts.

FOREMAN: Right. We have a job to do. Let's do it. Maybe if the gentleman who's disagreeing down there could tell us why. You know, tell us what he thinks—we could show him where he's probably mixed up.

11TH JUROR [*looking at the* 12TH JUROR's *doodle*]: What are you doing?

12TH JUROR: Mmm? Oh. [*He holds up the doodle.*] It's one of the products I work on at the ad agency. Rice Pops. "The Breakfast with the Built-in Bounce." I wrote that line.

11TH JUROR [*smiling in spite of himself*]: It's very catchy.

FOREMAN: If you don't mind!

The 2ND JUROR *rises, goes to the coat hooks and takes a package of cough drops from his jacket pocket.*

12TH JUROR: I'm sorry. I have this habit of doodling. It keeps me thinking clearly.

FOREMAN: We're trying to get someplace here. Y'know we can sit here forever . . .

12TH JUROR: Well, look, maybe this is an idea. I'm just thinking out loud, but it seems to me it's up to us to convince this gentleman—[*he indicates the* 8TH JUROR] that we're right and he's wrong. Maybe if we each took a minute or two. I mean, it's just a quick thought . . .

FOREMAN: No, I think it's a good one. Supposing we go once around the table in order of jury numbers.

7TH JUROR: Anything. Let's start it off.

FOREMAN: OK. [*To the* 2ND JUROR.] That means you're first.

2ND JUROR: Oh. Well . . . [*He pauses nervously.*] Well, it's hard to put into words. I just—think he's guilty. I thought it was obvious from the word go. I mean nobody proved otherwise.

8TH JUROR: Nobody has to prove otherwise. The burden of proof is on the prosecution. The defendant doesn't have to open his mouth. That's in the Constitution. You've heard of it.

2ND JUROR [*flustered*]: Well, sure I've heard of it. I know what it is. I—what I meant—well, the man is guilty. I mean, somebody saw him do it. [*He looks around helplessly.*]

3RD JUROR: OK. [*He refers to his notes.*] Now, here's what I think, and I have no personal feelings about this. I'm talking facts. Number one. Let's take the old man who lived on the second floor right underneath the room where the murder

took place. At ten minutes after twelve on the night of the
killing he heard loud noises in the apartment upstairs. He
said it sounded like a fight. Then he heard the kid shout out,
"I'm gonna kill you." A second later he heard a body fall and
he ran to the door of his apartment, looked out and saw the
kid running down the stairs and out of the house. Then he
called the police. They found the father with a knife in his
chest.

FOREMAN: And the coroner fixed the time of the death at
around midnight.

3RD JUROR: Right. I mean, there are facts for you. You can't
refute facts. This boy is guilty. Look, I'm as sentimental as
the next guy. I know the kid is only sixteen, but he's still got
to pay for what he did.

7TH JUROR: I'm with you, pops.

4TH JUROR [*removing his eyeglasses*]: It was obvious to me,
anyway, that the boy's entire story was flimsy. He claimed he
was at the movies during the time of the killing and yet one
hour later he couldn't remember what films he saw or who
played in them.

3RD JUROR: That's right. Did you hear that? [*To the* 4TH JU-
ROR.] You're absolutely right.

4TH JUROR: No one saw him going into or out of the theater.

10TH JUROR: Listen, what about that woman across the street?
If her testimony don't prove it, nothing does.

11TH JUROR: That's right. She was the one who actually saw
the killing.

FOREMAN [*half rising*]: Let's go in order here.

10TH JUROR [*rising, handkerchief in hand*]: Just a minute.
Here's a woman . . . [*He blows his nose.*] Here's a woman
who's lying in bed and can't sleep. She's dying with the heat.
Know what I mean? Anyway, she looks out the window and
right across the street she sees the kid stick the knife into his
father. The time is twelve ten on the nose. Everything fits.
Look, she's known the kid all his life. His window is right op-
posite hers, across the el tracks, and she swore she saw him
do it.

8TH JUROR: Through the windows of a passing elevated train.

10TH JUROR: Right. This el train had no passengers on it. It was just being moved downtown. The lights were out, remember? And they proved in court that at night you can look through the windows of an el train when the lights are out and see what's happening on the other side. They proved it.

8TH JUROR [*to the* 10TH JUROR]: I'd like to ask you something.

10TH JUROR: Sure.

8TH JUROR: You don't believe the boy. How come you believe the woman? She's one of "them," too, isn't she?

10TH JUROR [*suddenly angry*]: You're a pretty smart fellow, aren't you?

The 10TH JUROR *crosses toward the* 8TH JUROR. *Several* JURORS *rise as if to intercept the* 10TH JUROR.

FOREMAN: Hey, let's take it easy.

10TH JUROR [*angrily*]: What's he so wise about? I'm telling you . . .

3RD JUROR: Come on. Sit down. What are you letting him get you all upset for?

The 10TH JUROR *sits.*

FOREMAN: Let's calm down now. Let's try to keep it peaceful in here. Whose turn is it? [*To the* 5TH JUROR.] OK. How about you?

5TH JUROR [*looking nervously around*]: I'll pass it.

FOREMAN: That's your privilege. How about the next gentleman?

6TH JUROR: I don't know. I started to be convinced, uh—you know, very early in the case. Well, I was looking for the motive. That's very important. If there's no motive, where's the case? So anyway, that testimony from those people across the hall from the kid's apartment, that was very powerful. Didn't they say something about an argument between the father and the boy around seven o'clock that night? I mean, I can be wrong.

11TH JUROR: It was eight o'clock. Not seven.

8TH JUROR: That's right. Eight o'clock. They heard an argument, but they couldn't hear what it was about. Then they heard the father hit the boy twice, and finally they saw the boy walk angrily out of the house. What does that prove?

6TH JUROR: Well, it doesn't exactly prove anything. It's just part of the picture. I didn't say it proved anything.

8TH JUROR: You said it revealed a motive for the killing. The prosecuting attorney said the same thing. Well, I don't think it's a very strong motive. This boy has been hit so many times in his life that violence is practically a normal state of affairs for him. I can't see two slaps in the face provoking him into committing murder.

4TH JUROR [*quietly*]: It may have been two slaps too many. Everyone has a breaking point.

FOREMAN [*to the* 6TH JUROR.]: Anything else?

6TH JUROR: No.

FOREMAN: OK. [*To the* 7TH JUROR.] How about the next gentleman?

7TH JUROR: Me? [*He pauses, looks around, shrugs.*] I don't know, it's practically all said already. We can talk about it forever. I mean, this kid is oh for five. Look at his record. He was in Children's Court when he was ten for throwing a rock at his teacher. At fourteen he was in Reform School. He stole a car. He's been arrested for mugging. He was picked up twice for trying to slash another teenager with a knife. He's real quick with switch knives, they said. This is a very fine boy.

8TH JUROR: Ever since he was five years old his father beat him up regularly. He used his fists.

7TH JUROR: So would I. A kid like that.

4TH JUROR: Wouldn't you call those beatings a motive for him to kill his father?

8TH JUROR [*after a pause*]: I don't know. It's a motive for him to be an angry kid. I'll say that.

3RD JUROR: It's the kids, the way they are nowadays. Angry! Hostile! You can't do a damn thing with them. Just the way they talk to you. Listen, when I was his age I used to call my father "Sir." That's right, "Sir!" You ever hear a boy call his father that anymore?

8TH JUROR: Fathers don't seem to think it's important anymore.

3RD JUROR: No? Have you got any kids?

8TH JUROR: Two.

3RD JUROR: Yeah, well I've got one. He's twenty. We did

everything for that boy, and what happened? When he was nine he ran away from a fight. I saw him. I was so ashamed I almost threw up. So I told him right out. "I'm gonna make a man outa you or I'm gonna bust you in half trying." Well, I made a man outa him all right. When he was sixteen we had a battle. He hit me in the face. He's big, y'know. I haven't seen him in two years. Rotten kid. You work your heart out . . . [*He breaks off. He has said more than he intended. He is embarrassed.*] All right. Let's get on with it.

4TH JUROR [*rising*]: I think we're missing the point here. This boy, let's say he's a product of a filthy neighborhood and a broken home. We can't help that. We're here to decide whether he's guilty or innocent of murder, not to go into reasons why he grew up this way. He was born in a slum. Slums are breeding grounds for criminals. I know it. So do you. It's no secret. Children from slum backgrounds are potential menaces to society. Now I think—

10TH JUROR [*interrupting*]: Brother, you can say that again. The kids who crawl outa those places are real trash. I don't want any part of them, I'm telling you.

5TH JUROR [*rising*]: I've lived in a slum all my life. I nurse that trash in Harlem Hospital six nights a week.

10TH JUROR: Oh, now wait a second . . .

5TH JUROR: I used to play in a backyard that was filled with garbage. Maybe it still smells on me.

10TH JUROR [*his anger rising*]: Now listen, buddy.

FOREMAN [*to the* 5TH JUROR]: Now, let's be reasonable. There's nothing personal . . .

5TH JUROR [*loudly*]: There is something personal!
The 3RD JUROR *moves to the* 5TH JUROR *and pats him on the shoulder. The* 5TH JUROR *does not look up.*

3RD JUROR: Come on, now. He didn't mean you, feller. Let's not be so sensitive.

11TH JUROR: This sensitivity I understand.

FOREMAN: All right, let's stop all this arguing. We're wasting time here. [*He points to the* 8TH JUROR.] It's your turn. Let's go.

8TH JUROR: Well, I didn't expect a turn. I thought you were all supposed to be convincing me. Wasn't that the idea?

FOREMAN: Check. I forgot that.

10TH JUROR: Well, what's the difference? He's the one who's keeping us here. Let's hear what he's got to say.

FOREMAN: Now just a second. We decided to do it a certain way. Let's stick to what we said.

10TH JUROR [disgusted]: Ah, stop bein' a kid, will you?

FOREMAN: A kid! Listen, what d'you mean by that?

10TH JUROR: What d'ya think I mean? K-I-D, kid!

FOREMAN: What, just because I'm trying to keep this thing organized? Listen. [He rises.] You want to do it? Here. You sit here. You take the responsibility. I'll just shut up, that's all.

10TH JUROR: Listen, what are you gettin' so hot about? Calm down, will ya?

FOREMAN: Don't tell me to calm down. Here! Here's the chair. You keep it goin' smooth and everything. What d'ya think, it's a snap? Come on. Mr. Foreman. Let's see how great you'd run the show.

10TH JUROR [to the 11TH JUROR]: Did y'ever see such a thing?

FOREMAN: You think it's funny or something?

12TH JUROR: Take it easy. The whole thing's unimportant.

FOREMAN: Unimportant? You want to try it?

12TH JUROR: No. Listen, you're doing a beautiful job. Nobody wants to change.

7TH JUROR: Yeah, you're doing great. Hang in there and pitch.

10TH JUROR: All right. Let's hear from somebody.

There is a pause.

8TH JUROR: Well, if you want me to tell you how I feel about it right now, it's all right with me.

FOREMAN [softly]: I don't care what you do.

8TH JUROR [after a pause]: All right. I haven't got anything brilliant. I only know as much as you do. According to the testimony the boy looks guilty. Maybe he is. I sat there in court for three days listening while the evidence built up. Everybody sounded so positive that I started to get a peculiar feeling about this trial. I mean, nothing is that positive. I had questions I would have liked to ask. Maybe they wouldn't have meant anything. I don't know. But I started to feel that the defense counsel wasn't doing his job. He let too many things go. Little things.

10TH JUROR: What little things? Listen, when these guys don't ask questions, that's because they know the answers already and they figure they'll be hurt.

8TH JUROR: Maybe. It's also possible for a lawyer to be just plain stupid, isn't it?

6TH JUROR: You sound like you've met my brother-in-law.

A few of the JURORS *laugh.*

8TH JUROR [*smiling*]: I kept putting myself in the boy's place. I would have asked for another lawyer, I think. I mean, if I was on trial for my life I'd want my lawyer to tear the prosecution witnesses to shreds, or at least to try. Look, there was one alleged eyewitness to this killing. Someone else claims he heard the killing and then saw the boy running out afterward. There was a lot of circumstantial evidence, but actually those two witnesses were the entire case for the prosecution. Supposing they were wrong?

12TH JUROR: What do you mean, "Supposing they were wrong?" What's the point of having witnesses at all?

8TH JUROR: Could they be wrong?

12TH JUROR: They sat on the stand under oath. What are you trying to say?

8TH JUROR: They're only people. People make mistakes. Could they be wrong?

12TH JUROR: I . . . No! I don't think so.

8TH JUROR: Do you know so?

12TH JUROR: Well, now, listen. Nobody can know a thing like that. This isn't an exact science.

8TH JUROR: That's right. It isn't.

3RD JUROR [*rising angrily*]: All right. [*To the* 8TH JUROR.] Let's try to get to the point here. What about the switch knife they found in the father's chest?

2ND JUROR: Well, wait a minute. I think we oughta . . . There are some people who haven't talked yet. Shouldn't we . . . ?

3RD JUROR: Look, they can talk whenever they like. Now just be quiet a second, will you? [*He turns to the* 8TH JUROR.]

OK, what about the knife? You know, the one that fine, upright boy admitted buying on the night of the murder. Let's talk about that.

8TH JUROR: All right, let's talk about it. Let's get it in here and look at it. I'd like to see it again. [*He turns to the* FOREMAN.] Mr. Foreman?

The FOREMAN *rises and crosses to the door.*

3RD JUROR: We all know what it looks like.

The FOREMAN *knocks on the door.*

The GUARD *unlocks the door and enters.*

The FOREMAN *whispers to him.*

The GUARD *nods and exits, locking the door.*

What are we gonna get out of seeing it again?

5TH JUROR: You brought it up.

4TH JUROR: The gentleman has a right to see exhibits in evidence. [*To the* 8TH JUROR.] The knife, and the way it was bought, is pretty strong evidence. Don't you think so?

8TH JUROR: I do.

4TH JUROR: Good. Now suppose we take these facts one at a time. One. The boy admitted going out of his house at eight o'clock on the night of the murder after being punched several times by his father.

8TH JUROR: He didn't say "punched." He said "hit." There's a difference between a slap and a punch.

4TH JUROR: After being hit several times by his father. Two. The boy went directly to a neighborhood junk shop where he bought a . . . What do you call these things—

3RD JUROR ⎫   ⎧ Switch knives.
          ⎬ [together]: ⎨
4TH JUROR ⎭   ⎩ —a switchblade knife. [*To the* 3RD JUROR.] Thank you.

4TH JUROR: Three. This wasn't what you'd call an ordinary knife. It had a very unusual carved handle. Four. The storekeeper who sold it to him identified the knife in court and said it was the only one of its kind he had ever had in stock. Five. At, oh, about eight forty-five the boy ran into three friends of his in front of a diner. Am I correct so far?

8TH JUROR: Yes, you are.

3RD JUROR [*to the* 8TH JUROR]: You bet he is. [*To the others.*] Now, listen to this man. He knows what he's talking about.

4TH JUROR: The boy talked with his friends for about an hour, leaving them at nine forty-five. During this time they saw the switch knife. Six. Each of them identified the death weapon in court as that same knife. Seven. The boy arrived home at about ten o'clock. Now this is where the stories offered by the boy and the State begin to diverge slightly. He claims that he stayed home until eleven thirty and then went to one of those all-night movies. He returned home at about three fifteen in the morning to find his father dead and himself arrested. Now, what happened to the switch knife? This is the charming and imaginative little fable the boy invented. He claims that the knife fell through a hole in his pocket sometime between eleven thirty and three fifteen while he was on his trip to the movies and that he never saw it again. Now this is a tale, gentlemen. I think it's quite clear that the boy never went to the movies that night. No one in the house saw him go out at eleven thirty. No one at the theater identified him. He couldn't even remember the names of the pictures he saw. What actually happened is this: the boy stayed home, had another fight with this father, stabbed him to death with the knife at ten minutes after twelve and fled from the house. He even remembered to wipe the knife clean of fingerprints.

The GUARD *unlocks the door and enters carrying a curiously designed knife with a tag hanging from it.*

The 4TH JUROR *goes to the* GUARD, *and takes the knife from him.*

The GUARD *exits and locks the door.*

Everyone connected with the case identified the knife. Now are you trying to tell me that it really fell through a hole in the boy's pocket and that someone picked it up off the street, went to the boy's house and stabbed his father with it just to be amusing?

8TH JUROR: No. I'm saying it's possible that the boy lost the knife and that someone else stabbed his father with a similar knife. It's possible.

The 4TH JUROR *flicks open the knife and jams it into the table.*

4TH JUROR: Take a look at that knife. I've never seen one like it. Neither had the storekeeper who sold it to the boy. Aren't you asking us to accept a pretty incredible coincidence?

8TH JUROR: I'm not asking anyone to accept it. I'm just saying that it's possible.

3RD JUROR [*shouting*]: And I'm saying it's not possible.

The 8TH JUROR *stands for a moment in silence, then he reaches into his pocket and swiftly withdraws a knife. He holds it in front of his face and flicks open the blade, then he leans forward and sticks the knife into the table alongside the other. They are exactly alike. There is a burst of sound in the room. The* 8TH JUROR *stands back from the table, watching.*

6TH JUROR: Look at it! It's the same knife.

7TH JUROR: What is this?

12TH JUROR: Where'd that come from?

2ND JUROR: How d'you like that?

3RD JUROR [*looking at the* 8TH JUROR; *amazed*]: What are you trying to do?

10TH JUROR: Yeah. What's going on here? Who do you think you are?

4TH JUROR: Quiet! Let's be quiet. [*To the* 8TH JUROR.] Where d'you get that knife?

8TH JUROR: I was walking for a couple of hours last night, just thinking. I walked through the boy's neighborhood. The knife comes from a little pawnshop three blocks from his house. It cost six dollars.

4TH JUROR: It's against the law to buy or sell switchblade knives.

8TH JUROR: That's right. I broke the law.

3RD JUROR: Listen. You pulled a real bright trick here. Now, supposing you tell me what you proved. Maybe there are ten knives like that. So what?

8TH JUROR: Maybe there are.

3RD JUROR: So what does that mean? It's the same kind of knife. So what's that? The discovery of the age or something?

11TH JUROR: It would still be an incredible coincidence for another person to have stabbed the father with the same kind of knife.

3RD JUROR: That's right! He's right.

7TH JUROR: The odds are a million to one.

8TH JUROR: It's possible.

4TH JUROR: But not very probable.

FOREMAN: Listen, let's take seats. There's no point in milling round here.

They begin to move back to their seats. The 8TH JUROR *stands watching.*

2ND JUROR: It's interesting that he'd find a knife exactly like the one the boy bought.

3RD JUROR: What's interesting? You think it proves anything?

2ND JUROR: Well, no. I was just—

3RD JUROR: Interesting! [*He points at the* 8TH JUROR.] Listen, how come the kid bought the knife to begin with?

8TH JUROR: Well, he claims that—

3RD JUROR: I know. He claims he bought it as a present for a friend of his. He was gonna give it to him the next day because he busted the other kid's knife dropping it on the pavement.

8TH JUROR: That's what he said.

7TH JUROR: Baloney!

9TH JUROR: The friend testified that the boy did break his knife.

3RD JUROR: Yeah. And how long before the killing? Three weeks. Right? So how come our noble lad bought this knife one half-hour after his father smacked him and three and a half hours before they found it shoved up here in the father's chest?

7TH JUROR: Well, he was gonna give the knife to his friend. He just wanted to use it for a minute.

There is scattered laughter.

8TH JUROR [*to the* 3RD JUROR]: Let me ask you this. It's one of the questions I wanted to ask in court. If the boy bought the knife to use on his father, how come he showed what was going to be the murder weapon to three friends of his just a couple of hours before the killing?

3RD JUROR: Listen, all of this is just talk. The boy lied and you know it.

8TH JUROR: He may have lied. [*To the* 10TH JUROR.] Do you think he lied?

10TH JUROR: Now that's a stupid question. Sure he lied.

8TH JUROR [*to the* 4TH JUROR]: Do you?

4TH JUROR: You know my answer. He lied.

8TH JUROR [*to the* 5TH JUROR]: Do you think he lied?

5TH JUROR: I'm not sure . . . [*He breaks off and looks nervously around.*]

3RD JUROR [*leaping into the breach*]: You're not sure about what? Now wait a second. [*To the* 8TH JUROR.] What are you, the kid's lawyer or something? Who do you think you are to start cross-examining us?

8TH JUROR: Isn't that what's supposed to happen in a jury room?

3RD JUROR: Listen, there are still eleven of us in here who think he's guilty.

7TH JUROR: Yeah. What do you think you're gonna accomplish? You're not gonna change anybody's mind. So if you want to be stubborn and hang this jury, go ahead. The kid'll be tried again and found guilty sure as he's born.

8TH JUROR: You're probably right.

7TH JUROR: So what are you gonna do about it? We can be here all night.

9TH JUROR: It's only one night. A boy may die.

7TH JUROR: Brother! Anybody got a deck of cards?

2ND JUROR [*to the* FOREMAN]: I don't think he ought to make a joke about it.

FOREMAN: What do you want me to do?

10TH JUROR: Listen, I don't see what all this stuff about the knife has to do with anything. Somebody saw the kid stab his father. What more do we need? I got three garages of mine going to pot while you're talking. Let's get done and get outa here.

11TH JUROR: The knife was very important to the district attorney. He spent one whole morning . . .

10TH JUROR: He's a fifteenth assistant, or something. What does he know?

FOREMAN: OK. I think we oughta get on with it now. These side arguments only slow us up. [*To the* 8TH JUROR.] What about it?

6TH JUROR [*to the* 8TH JUROR]: You're the only one.

8TH JUROR: I have a proposition to make to all of you. I want to call for a vote. I'd like you eleven men to vote by secret written ballot. I'll abstain. If there are still eleven votes for guilty, I won't stand alone. We'll take a guilty verdict in to the judge right now. But if anyone votes not guilty, we'll stay and talk this thing out. [*He pauses.*] Well, that's all. If you want to try it, I'm ready.

3RD JUROR: Well, finally you're behaving like a reasonable man.

12TH JUROR: Check. I'll buy that.

7TH JUROR: OK. Let's do it.

FOREMAN: That sounds fair.

Some of the JURORS *nod. The* 8TH JUROR *moves to the window.*

Anyone doesn't agree? OK. Pass these along. [*He passes out slips of paper.*]

The 8TH JUROR *stands watching the others. The* JURORS *pass the slips along. Finally each of them begins to write. Now some of them begin to fold their slips and pass them back to the* FOREMAN. *The* FOREMAN *stacks all the slips on the table in front of him. He picks up the first slip of paper, opens it and reads.*

"Guilty."

He opens and reads the other slips in turn.

"Guilty." "Guilty." "Guilty." "Guilty." "Guilty." "Guilty." "Guilty." "Guilty." "Not Guilty."

There is a babble of voices. The 8TH JUROR *relaxes, moves to his chair and sits.*

[*Reading the last slip.*] "Guilty."

10TH JUROR: Boy! How do you like that?

7TH JUROR: And another chap flips his goddamn wig!

10TH JUROR: All right, who was it? Come on. I want to know.

11TH JUROR: Excuse me. This was a secret ballot. We agreed on this.

3RD JUROR: Secret? What d'ya mean, secret? There are no secrets in a jury room. I know who it was. [*He crosses to the* 5TH JUROR.] Brother, you're really something! You come in here and you vote guilty like everybody else, and then this golden-voiced preacher over here starts to tear your heart out with stories about a poor little kid who just couldn't help becoming a murderer. So you change your vote. If that isn't the most sickening . . . Why don'tcha drop a quarter in his collection box?

5TH JUROR: Now wait a minute.

The 3RD JUROR *turns away.*

You can't talk to me like that!

The 3RD JUROR *turns to face him. The* 4TH JUROR *slips in between them and takes the* 5TH JUROR *by the arm.*

No. [*He shakes off the* 4TH JUROR.] Where does he get the right to shout at me?

4TH JUROR: All right, let's calm down.

5TH JUROR: Who does he think he is? I mean, did you see him?

4TH JUROR: Just sit down. He's very excitable. Forget it. It doesn't matter.

3RD JUROR: You bet I'm excitable. We're trying to put a guilty man into the chair where he belongs and all of a sudden somebody's telling us fairy tales—and we're listening.

2ND JUROR [*mildly*]: Take it easy.

3RD JUROR: What do you mean—take it easy! D'you feel like seeing a proven murderer walking the streets? Why don't we give him his knife back? Make it easier for him.

FOREMAN: OK, let's stop the yelling. Who's got something constructive to say?

11TH JUROR: Please. I would like to say something here. I have always thought that in this country a man was entitled to have unpopular opinions . . .

7TH JUROR: Let's stick to the subject. [*To the* 5TH JUROR.] What made you change your vote?

9TH JUROR: He didn't change his vote. I did. Would you like me to tell you why?

7TH JUROR: No, I wouldn't like you to tell me why.

9TH JUROR: Well, I'd like to make it clear, anyway, if you don't mind.

10TH JUROR: Do we have to listen to this?

6TH JUROR: Hey, look! The man wants to talk.

9TH JUROR: Thank you. [*To the* 7TH JUROR.] This gentleman— [*he indicates the* 8TH JUROR] has been standing alone against

us. He doesn't say the boy is not guilty. He just isn't sure.
Well, it's not easy to stand alone against the ridicule of others. He gambled for support and I gave it to him. I respect his
motives. The boy on trial is probably guilty. But I want to hear
more.

The 7TH JUROR crosses to the washroom.

For the time being the vote is ten to two.

The 7TH JUROR enters the washroom, slams the door after him.

I'm talking here. You have no right to . . .

8TH JUROR [*to the* 9TH JUROR]: He can't hear you. He never
will.

3RD JUROR: Well, if the speech is over, maybe we can go on.

FOREMAN: I think we ought to take a break. One man's inside
there. Let's wait for him.

*The FOREMAN moves above the table to where the two knives
are stuck into it. He plucks the tagged knife out and closes it.*

12TH JUROR [*to the* 11TH JUROR]: Looks like we're really hung
up here. I mean, that thing with the old man was pretty un-
expected. I wish I knew how we could break this up. [*He
smiles suddenly.*] Y'know, in advertising . . . I told you I
worked at an ad agency, didn't I?

The FOREMAN crosses to the door and knocks.

The GUARD unlocks the door and enters.

The FOREMAN hands him the knife.

The GUARD exits, locking the door.

Well, there are some pretty strange people—not strange,
really—they just have peculiar ways of expressing them-
selves, y'know what I mean?

The 11TH JUROR nods.

Well, it's probably the same in your business—right? What
do you do?

11TH JUROR: I'm a watchmaker.

12TH JUROR: Really? The finest watchmakers come from Eu-
rope, I imagine.

The 11TH JUROR bows slightly.

The 6TH JUROR rises, and goes into the lavatory.

Anyway, I was telling you—in the agency, when they reach a
point like this in a meeting, there's always some character

ready with an idea. And it kills me, I mean it's the weirdest thing sometimes the way they precede the idea with some kind of phrase. Like—oh, some account exec'll say, "Here's an idea. Let's run it up the flagpole and see if anyone salutes it," or "Put it on a bus and see if it gets off at Wall Street." I mean, it's idiotic, but it's funny.

The 8TH JUROR *goes into the washroom and hangs his jacket on a hook. The* 3RD JUROR *crosses to the* 5TH JUROR.

3RD JUROR [*to the* 5TH JUROR]: Look, I was a little excited. Well, you know how it is—I didn't mean to get nasty or anything.

The 5TH JUROR *crosses away from the* 3RD JUROR *without answering. The* 7TH JUROR *steps away from the washbasin and dries his hands. The* 8TH JUROR *crosses to the washbasin.*

7TH JUROR [*to the* 8TH JUROR]: Say, are you a salesman?

8TH JUROR: I'm an architect.

7TH JUROR: You know what the soft sell is? You're pretty good at it. I'll tell ya. I got a different technique. Jokes. Drinks. Knock 'em on their asses. I made twenty-seven thousand last year selling marmalade. That's not bad. Considering marmalade. [*He watches the* 8TH JUROR *for a moment.*] What are ya getting out of it—kicks? The boy is guilty, pal. So let's go home before we get sore throats.

8TH JUROR: What's the difference whether you get one here or at the ball game?

7TH JUROR: No difference pal. No difference at all.

The 7TH JUROR *goes back into the jury room.*

The 6TH JUROR *enters from the lavatory, goes to the washbasin and washes his hands.*

6TH JUROR [*to the* 8TH JUROR]: Nice bunch of guys.

8TH JUROR: I guess they're the same as any.

6TH JUROR: That loud, heavyset guy, the one who was tellin' us about his kid—the way he was talking—boy, that was an embarrassing thing.

8TH JUROR: Yeah.

6TH JUROR: What a murderous day. You think we'll be here much longer?

8TH JUROR: I don't know.

6TH JUROR: He's guilty for sure. There's not a doubt in the whole world. We shoulda been done already. Listen, I don't care, y'know. It beats workin'.

The 8TH JUROR *smiles.*

You think he's innocent?

8TH JUROR: I don't know. It's possible.

6TH JUROR: I don't know you, but I'm bettin' you've never been wronger in your life. Y'oughta wrap it up. You're wastin' your time.

8TH JUROR: Suppose you were the one on trial?

6TH JUROR: I'm not used to supposing. I'm just a working man. My boss does the supposing. But I'll try one. Suppose you talk us all outa this and the kid really did knife his father? *The* 6TH JUROR *looks at the* 8TH JUROR *for a moment, then goes into the jury room. The* 8TH JUROR *stands alone for a few moments and we know that this is the problem that has been tormenting him. He does not know, and never will. He switches out the washroom light and goes into the jury room.*

FOREMAN: OK, let's take seats.

2ND JUROR: Looks like we'll be here for dinner.

FOREMAN: OK. Let's get down to business. Who wants to start it off?

There is a pause, then the 4TH *and* 6TH JURORS *start to speak at the same time.*

6TH JUROR ⎫
             ⎬ (together): ⎰ Well, I'd like to make a
             ⎪   ⎪ point. (*To the* 4TH JUROR.)
             ⎪   ⎪ Pardon me.
4TH JUROR ⎭   ⎱ Maybe it would be profitable
                           if we . . . (*To the* 6TH JUROR.)
                           I'm sorry, go ahead.

6TH JUROR: I didn't mean to interrupt.

4TH JUROR: No. Go ahead. It's all right.

6TH JUROR: Well. I was going to say, well, this is probably a small point, but anyway . . . [*To the* 8TH JUROR.] The boy had a motive for the killing. You know, the beatings and all. So if he didn't do it, who did? Who else had the motive? That's my point. I mean, nobody goes out and kills someone without a motive, not unless he's just plain nuts. Right?

8TH JUROR: As far as I know, we're supposed to decide whether or not the boy on trial is guilty beyond a reasonable doubt. We're not concerned with anyone else's motives here. That's a job for the police.

4TH JUROR: Very true. But we can't help letting the only motive we know of creep into our thoughts, can we? And we can't help asking ourselves who else might have had a motive. Logically, these things follow. [*He nods toward the* 6TH JUROR.] This gentleman is asking a reasonable question. Somebody killed him. If it wasn't the boy, who was it?

3RD JUROR: Modjelewski.

7TH JUROR: You're talking about the man I love!

4TH JUROR: If you haven't got anything to add besides jokes, I suggest you listen.

3RD JUROR: OK. It's just letting off steam. I'm sorry. Go ahead.

4TH JUROR [*to the* 8TH JUROR]: Well, maybe you can answer me. Who else might have killed the father?

8TH JUROR: Well, I don't know. The father wasn't exactly a model citizen. The boy's lawyer outlined his background in his closing statement. He was in prison once. He was known to be a compulsive gambler and a pretty consistent loser. He spent a lot of time in neighborhood bars and he'd get into fistfights sometimes after a couple of drinks. Usually over a woman. He was a tough, cruel, primitive kind of man who never held a job for more than six months in his life. So here are a few possibilities. He could have been murdered by one of many men he served time with in prison. By a bookmaker. By a man he'd beaten up. By a woman he'd picked up. By any one of the people he was known to hang out with.

10TH JUROR: Boy-oh-boy, that's the biggest load of crap I ever . . . Listen, we know the father was a bum. So what has that got to do with anything?

8TH JUROR: I didn't bring it up. I was asked who else might have killed him. I gave my answer.

9TH JUROR [*pointing at the* 4TH JUROR]: That gentleman over there asked a direct question.

10TH JUROR: Everyone's a lawyer!

3RD JUROR: Look, suppose you answer this for me. The old

man who lived downstairs heard the kid yell out, "I'm going to kill you." A split second later he heard a body hit the floor. Then he saw the kid run out of the house. Now what does all that mean to you?

8TH JUROR: I was wondering how clearly the old man could have heard the boy's voice through the ceiling.

3RD JUROR: He didn't hear it through the ceiling. His window was open and so was the window upstairs. It was a hot night, remember?

8TH JUROR: The voice came from another apartment. It's not easy to identify a voice, especially a shouting voice.

FOREMAN: He identified it in court. He picked the boy's voice out of five other voices, blindfolded.

8TH JUROR: That was just an ambitious district attorney putting on a show. Look, the old man knows the boy's voice very well. They've lived in the same house for years. But to identify it positively from the apartment downstairs . . . Isn't it possible he was wrong—that maybe he thought the boy was upstairs and automatically decided that the voice he heard was the boy's voice?

4TH JUROR: I think that's a bit far-fetched.

10TH JUROR: Brother, you can say that again. [To the 8TH JUROR.] Look. The old man heard the father's body falling and then he saw the boy run out of the house fifteen seconds later. He saw the boy.

12TH JUROR: Check. And don't forget the woman across the street. She looked right into the open window and saw the boy stab his father. I mean, isn't that enough for you?

8TH JUROR: Not right now. No, it isn't.

7TH JUROR: How do you like him? It's like talking into a dead phone.

4TH JUROR: The woman saw the killing through the windows of a moving elevated train. The train had six cars and she saw it through the windows of the last two cars. She remembered the most insignificant details. I don't see how you can argue with that.

3RD JUROR [to the 8TH JUROR]: Well, what have you got to say about it?

8TH JUROR: I don't know. It doesn't sound right to me.

3RD JUROR: Well, suppose you think about it. [*To the* 12TH JUROR.] Lend me your pencil.

The 12TH JUROR *hands the pencil to the* 3RD JUROR, *who starts to draw what is obviously a tic-tac-toe pattern on the pad.*

8TH JUROR: I wonder if anybody has any idea how long it takes an elevated train . . .

The 8TH JUROR *sees the* 3RD JUROR *and the* 12TH JUROR *playing tic-tac-toe, snatches up the pad, tears off the top sheet, crumples it and drops it in the wastebasket.*

3RD JUROR: Wait a minute!

8TH JUROR: This isn't a game.

3RD JUROR [*shouting*]: Who do you think you are?

12TH JUROR [*to the* 3RD JUROR]: All right, take it easy.

FOREMAN: Come on now, sit down.

3RD JUROR: I've got a good mind to belt him one.

FOREMAN: Now, please! I don't want any fights in here.

3RD JUROR: Did you see him? The nerve! The absolute nerve!

10TH JUROR: All right. Forget it. It's not important. Know what I mean?

3RD JUROR: "This isn't a game." Who does he think he's dealing with here?

FOREMAN: Come on, now. It's all over. Let's take our seats.

3RD JUROR: What's all over? I want an apology.

6TH JUROR: OK, noisy. He apologizes. Now let's hear what the man has to say.

8TH JUROR: Thank you. I wonder if anybody has an idea how long it takes an elevated train going at medium speed to pass a given point?

7TH JUROR: What has that got to do with anything?

8TH JUROR: How long? Take a guess.

4TH JUROR: I wouldn't have the slightest idea.

8TH JUROR: [*to the* 5TH JUROR]: What do you think?

5TH JUROR: I don't know. About ten or twelve seconds, maybe.

3RD JUROR: What's all this for?

8TH JUROR: I'd say that was a fair guess. Anyone else?

11TH JUROR: That sounds right to me.

10TH JUROR: Come on, what's the guessing game for?

8TH JUROR [*to the* 2ND JUROR]: What would you say?

2ND JUROR: Ten seconds. Approximately.

4TH JUROR: All right. Say ten seconds. What are you getting at?

8TH JUROR: This. It takes a six-car el train ten seconds to pass a given point. Now say that given point is the open window of the room in which the killing took place. You can almost reach out the window of that room and touch the el tracks. Right?

5TH JUROR: Right.

8TH JUROR: All right. Now let me ask you this—has anyone here ever lived right next to the el tracks?

6TH JUROR: Well, I just finished painting an apartment that overlooked an el line. I'm a house painter, y'know. I was there for three days.

8TH JUROR: What was it like?

6TH JUROR: What d'ya mean?

8TH JUROR: Noisy?

6TH JUROR: Brother! Well, it didn't matter. We're all punchy in our business, anyway. [*He laughs.*]

8TH JUROR: I lived in a second-floor apartment next to an el line once. When the window's open and the train goes by, the noise is almost unbearable. You can't hear yourself think.

3RD JUROR: OK. You can't hear yourself think. Will you get to the point?

8TH JUROR: I will. Let's take two pieces of testimony and try to put them together. First, the old man in the apartment downstairs. He says he heard the boy say, "I'm going to kill you" and a split second later he heard the body hit the floor. One second later. Right?

2ND JUROR: That's right.

8TH JUROR: Second, the woman in the apartment across the street. She claimed that she looked out of her window and saw the killing through the last two cars of a passing elevated train. Right? The last two cars.

3RD JUROR: All right. What point are you making here?

8TH JUROR: Now, we agreed that an el train takes about ten seconds to pass a given point. Since the woman saw the stabbing through the last two cars, we can assume that the body fell to the floor just as the train passed by. Therefore, the el train had been roaring by the old man's window for a full ten seconds before the body fell. The old man, according to his own testimony, hearing "I'm going to kill you" and the body falling a split second later, would have had to hear the boy make this statement while the el was roaring past his nose. It's not possible that he could have heard it.

3RD JUROR: That's idiotic! Sure he could have heard it.

8TH JUROR: [*to the* 3RD JUROR]: Do you think so?

3RD JUROR: The old man said the boy yelled it out. That's enough for me.

8TH JUROR: If he heard anything at all, he still couldn't have identified the voice with the el roaring by.

3RD JUROR: You're talking about a matter of seconds here. Nobody can be that accurate.

8TH JUROR: Well, I think that testimony that could put a human being into the electric chair should be that accurate.

5TH JUROR: I don't think he could have heard it.

6TH JUROR: Yeah. Maybe he didn't hear it. I mean, with the el noise . . .

3RD JUROR: What are you people talking about?

5TH JUROR: Well, it stands to reason . . .

3RD JUROR: You're crazy! Why should he lie? What's he got to gain?

9TH JUROR: Attention, maybe.

3RD JUROR: You keep coming up with these bright sayings. Why don't you send one in to a newspaper? They pay three dollars.

6TH JUROR [*to the* 3RD JUROR]: Hey! What're ya talking to him like that for?

The 3RD JUROR *looks at the* 6TH JUROR, *then turns disgustedly away. The* 6TH JUROR *reaches out and turns the* 3RD JUROR *firmly around by the arm.*

A guy who talks like that to an old man oughta really get stepped on y'know.

3RD JUROR: Get your hands off me!

6TH JUROR: You oughta have some respect, mister. If you say stuff like that to him again—I'm gonna lay you out.

The 6TH JUROR *releases the* 3RD JUROR *and speaks to the* 9TH
JUROR.
Go ahead. You can say anything you want. Why do you think
the old man might lie?

9TH JUROR: It's just that I looked at him for a very long time.
The seam of his jacket was split under his arm. Did you no-
tice it? I mean, to come into court like that. He was a very old
man with a torn jacket and he walked very slowly to the
stand. He was dragging his left leg and trying to hide it because he was ashamed. I think I know him better than anyone here. This is a quiet, frightened, insignificant old man
who has been nothing all his life, who has never had recogni-
tion, his name in the newspapers. Nobody knows him, nobody quotes him, nobody seeks his advice after seventy-five
years. That's a very sad thing, to be nothing. A man like this
needs to be recognized, to be listened to, to be quoted just
once. This is very important. It would be so hard for him to
recede into the background . . .

7TH JUROR: Now, wait a minute. Are you trying to tell us he'd
lie just so that he could be important once?

9TH JUROR: No. He wouldn't really lie. But perhaps he'd
make himself believe that he'd heard those words and recognized the boy's face.

10TH JUROR: Well, that's the most fantastic story I've ever
heard. How can you make up a thing like that? What do you
know about it?

The 9TH JUROR *lowers his head, embarrassed.*

4TH JUROR: Gentlemen, this case is based on a reasonable and
logical progression of facts. Let's keep it there.

11TH JUROR: Facts may be colored by the personalities of the
people who present them.

2ND JUROR: Anybody want a cough drop?

10TH JUROR: I'll take one.

The 2ND JUROR *offers the cough drops to the* 10TH JUROR.
The 10TH JUROR *takes one.*
Thanks.

12TH JUROR: Say what you like, I still don't see how anybody
can think the boy's not guilty.

8TH JUROR: There's another thing I wanted to talk about for a minute. I think we've proved that the old man couldn't have heard the boy say, "I'm going to kill you," but supposing—

10TH JUROR: You didn't prove it at all. What are you talking about?

8TH JUROR: But supposing he really did hear it. This phrase, how many times has each of us used it? Probably hundreds. "I could kill you for that, darling." "If you do that once more, Junior, I'm going to kill you." "Come on, Rocky, kill him." We say it every day. It doesn't mean we're going to kill someone.

3RD JUROR: Wait a minute! What are you trying to give us here? The phrase was, "I'm going to kill you," and the kid screamed it out at the top of his lungs. Don't tell me he didn't mean it. Anybody says a thing like that the way he said it, they mean it.

2ND JUROR: Well, gee, I don't know. I remember I was arguing with the guy I work next to at the bank a couple of weeks ago; so he called me an idiot; so I yelled at him . . .

3RD JUROR: No listen, this guy is making you believe things that aren't so. The kid said he was going to kill him and he did kill him.

8TH JUROR: Well, let me ask you this: do you really think the boy would shout out a thing like that so the whole neighborhood would hear it? I don't think so. He's much too bright for that.

10TH JUROR: Bright? He's a common, ignorant slob. He don't even speak good English.

11TH JUROR: He doesn't even speak good English.

5TH JUROR: I'd like to change my vote to "not guilty."

7TH JUROR: Now you've got to be kidding.

5TH JUROR: You heard.

FOREMAN: Are you sure?

5TH JUROR: Yes, I'm sure.

FOREMAN: The vote is nine to three in favor of "guilty."

7TH JUROR: Well, if that isn't the livin' end! What are you basing it on? Stories this guy made up. He oughta write for *Amazing Detective Monthly*. He'd make a fortune. [*To the* 5TH

JUROR.] Listen, there are facts staring you right in your face.
Every one of them says this kid killed his old man. For cryin'
out loud, his own lawyer knew he didn't stand a chance right
from the beginning. His own lawyer. You could see it. He deserves the chair.

8TH JUROR: Does he? It's happened before that someone's been
convicted of murder and executed, and years later someone
else has confessed to the crime. Sometimes . . . sometimes the
facts that are staring you in the face are wrong!

7TH JUROR [to the 8TH JUROR]: I'm talkin' to him—[he indicates the 5TH JUROR] not to you. [To the others.] Boy, this
guy is really something. [To the 8TH JUROR.] Listen, the kid
had a lawyer, didn't he? The lawyer presented his case, not
you. How come you've got so much to say?

8TH JUROR: The lawyer was court-appointed.

7TH JUROR: So what does that mean?

8TH JUROR: Well, it could mean a lot of things. It could mean
he didn't want the case. It could mean he resented being ap-
pointed. It's the kind of case that brings him nothing. No
money. No glory. Not even much chance of winning. It's not
a very promising situation for a young lawyer. He'd really
have to believe in his client to make a good fight. As you
pointed out a minute ago, he obviously didn't.

7TH JUROR: Sure he didn't. Who in hell could, except God
come to earth or somebody? [He looks at his watch then up
at the clock.] Come on already! Look at the time!

11TH JUROR: Pardon me, but I have made some notes here.

10TH JUROR: Notes yet!

11TH JUROR: I would like please to say something. I have been
listening very closely, and it seems to me that this man—[he
indicates the 8TH JUROR] has some very good points to make.
From what was presented at the trial the boy looks guilty, but
maybe if we go deeper—

10TH JUROR: Come on, will ya?

11TH JUROR: There is a question I would like to ask. We assume that the boy committed murder. He stabbed his father
in the chest and ran away. This was at ten minutes after twelve.
Now, how was he caught by the police? He came home at

three o'clock or so and was captured by two detectives in the hallway of his house. My question is, if he really had killed his father, why would he come back three hours later? Wouldn't he be afraid of being caught?

3RD JUROR: Look—he came home to get his knife. It's not nice to leave knives sticking around in people's chests.

7TH JUROR: Yeah, especially relatives'.

4TH JUROR [to the 11TH JUROR]: The boy knew that there were people who could identify the knife as the one he had just bought. He had to get it before the police did.

11TH JUROR: But if he knew the knife could be identified, why did he leave it there in the first place?

4TH JUROR: Well, I think we can assume he ran out in a state of panic after he killed his father, and then when he finally calmed down, he realized that he had left the knife there.

11TH JUROR: This then depends on your definition of panic. He was calm enough to see to it that there were no fingerprints on the knife. Now where did his panic start and where did it end?

3RD JUROR: Look, you can forget all that other stuff. He still came home to dig out his knife and get rid of it.

11TH JUROR: Three hours later?

3RD JUROR: Sure, three hours later.

11TH JUROR: If I were the boy and I had killed my father, I would not have come home three hours later. I would be afraid that the police would be there. I would stay away, knife or no knife.

3RD JUROR: Listen, you voted "guilty," didn't you? What side are you on?

11TH JUROR: I don't believe I have to be loyal to one side or the other. I am simply asking questions.

12TH JUROR: Well, this is just off the top of my head, but if I were the boy, and I'd, you know, done the stabbing and everything, I'd take a chance and go back for the knife. I'll bet he figured no one had seen him and that the body probably wasn't even discovered yet. After all, it was the middle of the night. He probably thought no one would find the body till the next day.

11TH JUROR: Pardon. Here is my whole point. The woman across the street testified that a moment after she saw the killing, that is, a moment after the el train went by, she screamed and then went to telephone the police. Now, the boy must certainly have heard that scream and known that somebody saw something. I don't think he would have gone back if he had been the murderer.

4TH JUROR: Two points. One: in his state of panic he may not have heard the scream. Perhaps it wasn't very loud. Two: if he did hear it, he may not have connected it with his own act. Remember, he lived in a neighborhood where screams were fairly commonplace.

3RD JUROR: Right! There's your answer.

8TH JUROR: Maybe. Maybe he did stab his father, didn't hear the woman's screams, did run out in a panic, did calm down three hours later and came back to try and get the knife, risking being caught by the police. Maybe all those things are so. But maybe they're not. I think there's enough doubt to make us wonder whether he was there at all during the time the murder took place.

10TH JUROR: What d'ya mean doubt? What are you talking about? Didn't the old man see him running out of the house? He's twisting the facts. I'm telling you! [*To the* 11TH JUROR.] Did or didn't the old man see the kid running out of the house at twelve ten? Well, did he or didn't he?

11TH JUROR: He says he did.

10TH JUROR: Says he did! [*To the others.*] Boy-oh-boy! How do you like that? [*To the* 11TH JUROR.] Well, did or didn't the woman across the street see the kid kill his father? She says she did. You're makin' out like it don't matter what people say. What you want to believe, you believe, and what you don't want to believe, you don't. What kind of way is that? What d'ya think these people get up on the witness stand for—their health? I'm telling you men the facts are being changed around here. Witnesses are being doubted and there's no reason for it.

5TH JUROR: Witnesses can make mistakes.

10TH JUROR: Sure, when you want 'em to, they do! Know what I mean?

FOREMAN: OK. Let's hold the yelling down.

10TH JUROR: You keep saying that. Maybe what we need is a little yelling in here. These guys are going off every which way. Did hear the scream, didn't hear the scream. What's the difference? They're just little details. You're forgetting the important stuff. I mean, all of a sudden here everybody . . .

8TH JUROR: I'd like to call for another vote.

10TH JUROR: Listen, I'm talking here.

FOREMAN: There's another vote called for. How about taking seats?

Jurors who are standing move toward their seats.

3RD JUROR: What are we gonna gain by voting again?

FOREMAN: I don't know. The gentleman asked . . .

3RD JUROR: I never saw so much time spent on nothing.

2ND JUROR: [*mildly*]: It only takes a second.

FOREMAN: OK. I guess the fastest way is to find out who's voting not guilty. All those in favor of "not guilty" raise their hands.

The 5TH, 8TH, and 9TH JURORS raise their hands.

Still the same. One, two, three "not guiltys." Nine "guiltys."

7TH JUROR: So now where are we? I'm telling you, we can yakety-yak until next Tuesday here. Where's it getting us?

11TH JUROR: Pardon. [*He slowly raises his hand.*] I vote "not guilty."

7TH JUROR: Oh, brother!

3RD JUROR: Oh, now listen! What are you talking about? I mean, we're all going crazy in here or something! This kid is guilty. Why don'tcha pay attention to the facts. [*To the 4TH JUROR.*] Listen, tell him, will ya? This is getting to be a goddamn joke!

FOREMAN: The vote is eight to four, in favor of "guilty."

3RD JUROR: I mean, everybody's heart is starting to bleed for this punk little kid like the President just declared it "Love Your Underprivileged Brother Week" or something. [*To the 11TH JUROR.*] Listen, I'd like you to tell me why you changed your vote. Come on, give me reasons.

11TH JUROR: I don't have to defend my decision to you. I have a reasonable doubt in my mind.

3RD JUROR: What reasonable doubt? That's nothing but words. [*He pulls out the switch knife from the table and holds it up.*] Here, look at this. The kid you just decided isn't guilty was seen ramming this thing into his father. Well, look at it, Mr. Reasonable Doubt.

9TH JUROR: That's not the knife. Don't you remember?

3RD JUROR: Brilliant! [*He sticks the knife into the table.*]

7TH JUROR: I'm tellin' ya, this is the craziest. [*To the* 8TH JUROR.] I mean, you're sittin' in here pulling stories outa thin air. What're we supposed to believe? [*To the others.*] I'm telling you, if this guy was sitting ringside at the Dempsey-Firpo fight, he'd be tryin' to tell us Firpo won. [*To the* 8TH JUROR.] Look, what about the old man? Are we supposed to believe that he didn't get up and run to his door and see the kid tearing down the stairs fifteen seconds after the killing? He's only saying he did to be important. I mean, what's the point of the whole—?

5TH JUROR: Hold it a second.

7TH JUROR: And the Milwaukee rooter is heard from.

5TH JUROR: Did the old man say he ran to the door?

7TH JUROR: Ran. Walked. What's the difference? He got there.

6TH JUROR: He said he ran to the door. At least, I think he did.

5TH JUROR: I don't remember what he said. But I don't see how he could run.

4TH JUROR: He said he went from his bedroom to the front door. That's enough, isn't it?

8TH JUROR: Wait a minute. Where was his bedroom, again?

10TH JUROR: Down the hall somewhere. I thought you remembered everything. Don't you remember that?

8TH JUROR: No. Mr. Foreman, I'd like to take a look at the diagram of the apartment.

7TH JUROR: Why don't we have them run the trial over just so you can get everything straight?

8TH JUROR: Mr. Foreman . . .

FOREMAN: I heard you.

The FOREMAN *goes to the door and knocks.*

The GUARD *unlocks the door and enters.*

The FOREMAN *confers briefly with him.*

The GUARD *exits and locks the door after him.*

3RD JUROR: All right, what's this for? How come you're the only one in the room who wants to see exhibits all the time?

5TH JUROR: I want to see this one too.

3RD JUROR: And I want to stop wasting time.

4TH JUROR: If we're going to start wading through all that business about where the body was found . . .

8TH JUROR: We're not. Not unless someone else wants to. I'd like to see if a very old man who drags one leg when he walks because he had a stroke last year can get from his bed to his front door in fifteen seconds.

3RD JUROR: He said twenty seconds.

8TH JUROR: He said fifteen.

3RD JUROR: Now I'm telling you he said twenty. What're you trying to distort . . .

11TH JUROR: He said fifteen.

3RD JUROR: How does he know how long fifteen seconds is? You can't judge that kind of thing.

9TH JUROR: He said fifteen seconds. He was very positive about it.

3RD JUROR: He's an old man. You saw him. Half the time he was confused. How could he be positive about anything?

The GUARD *unlocks the door and enters, carrying a large diagram of the apartment.*

The diagram is a layout of a railroad flat. A bedroom faces the el tracks. Behind it is a series of rooms off a long hall. In the front room is an X marking the spot where the body was found. At the back of the apartment we see the entrance into the apartment hall from the building hall. We see a flight of stairs in the building's hall. Each room is labelled and the dimensions of each room are shown. The FOREMAN *takes the diagram.*

The GUARD *exits and locks the door.*

12TH JUROR: I don't see what we're going to prove here. The man said he saw the boy running out.

8TH JUROR: Well, let's see if the details bear him out. As soon

as the body fell to the floor, he said, he heard footsteps upstairs running toward the front door. He heard the upstairs
door open and the footsteps start down the stairs. He got to
his front door as soon as he could. He swore that it couldn't
have been more than fifteen seconds. Now, if the killer began
running immediately—

12TH JUROR: Well, maybe he didn't.

8TH JUROR: The old man said he did.

7TH JUROR: You know, you ought to be down in Atlantic City
at that hairsplitters' convention.

6TH JUROR: Listen, baseball, why don't you stop making
smart remarks all the time?

7TH JUROR: My friend, for your three dollars a day you've
gotta listen to everything.

10TH JUROR: [to the 8TH JUROR]: Well, now that you've got
that thing in here, what about it?

8TH JUROR [to the FOREMAN]: May I? [He takes the plan and
puts it on a chair.] This is the apartment in which the killing
took place. The old man's apartment is directly beneath it and
exactly the same. Here are the el tracks. The bedroom. Another
bedroom. Bathroom. Living room. Kitchen. And this is the
hall. Here's the front door to the apartment. And here are the
stairs. Now, the old man was in bed in this room. [He indicates
the front bedroom.] He says he got up, went out into the hall,
down the hall to the front door, opened it and looked out just
in time to see the boy racing down the stairs. Am I right so far?

3RD JUROR: That's the story, for the nineteenth time.

8TH JUROR: Fifteen seconds after he heard the body fall.

11TH JUROR: Correct.

8TH JUROR: His bed was at the window. It's [He looks closely
at the plan.] twelve feet from his bed to the bedroom door.
The length of the hall is forty-three feet, six inches. Now he
had to get up out of bed, walk twelve feet, open the bedroom
door, walk forty-three feet and open the front door—all in
fifteen seconds. Do you think he could have done it?

10TH JUROR: Sure he coulda done it.

11TH JUROR: He can only walk very slowly. They had to help
him into the witness chair.

3RD JUROR: You make it sound like a long walk. It's not.

9TH JUROR: For an old man who had a stroke it's a long walk.
The 8TH JUROR *moves his chair and sets the chair to indicate a bed.*

8TH JUROR: This is the old man's bed.

10TH JUROR: What's going on here?

8TH JUROR: I want to try this thing. Let's see how long it took him.

3RD JUROR: What d'you mean you want to try it? Why didn't the kid's lawyer bring it up, if it's so important?

5TH JUROR: Well, maybe he just didn't think of it.

10TH JUROR: What d'ya mean, he didn't think of it? You think the man's an idiot or something. It's an obvious thing.

5TH JUROR: Did you think of it?

10TH JUROR: Listen, smart guy. It don't matter whether I thought of it.

FOREMAN: OK, now . . . let's hold it down.

10TH JUROR: He didn't bring it up because he knew the answer'd hurt his case. Now what d'ya think of that?

FOREMAN: OK.

8TH JUROR: All right, here's the bed. I'm going to pace off twelve feet, the length of the bedroom. [*He paces twelve feet.*]

3RD JUROR: You're crazy. You can't re-create a thing like that.

11TH JUROR: I'd like to see it.
The 12TH JUROR *picks up his chair and takes it to the* 8TH JUROR. *The* 8TH JUROR *puts the chair where he is standing.*

8TH JUROR: All right, this is the bedroom door. The hall is a little over forty-three feet long. I'll pace over to that wall and back again.
The 8TH JUROR *paces, counting his steps silently.*

10TH JUROR: Look, this is absolutely insane. What's the idea of wasting everybody's time here?

8TH JUROR: . . . twelve . . . [*He stops and turns to the* 10TH JUROR.] According to you it'll only take fifteen seconds. We can spare that. [*He resumes his pacing, counting to himself, and reaches the wall.*]
The others watch silently.

[*He turns and paces, counting off the rest of the distance.*] . . . thirty-nine, forty, forty-one, forty-two, forty-three. OK, pass me another chair, please.

The 6TH JUROR *picks up a chair and takes it to the* 8TH JU-ROR. *The* 8TH JUROR *places it where he is standing.*

This is the door to the outside hall and stairway. It was chain-locked according to the testimony. Who's got a watch with a second hand?

2ND JUROR: I have.

8TH JUROR: When you want me to start, stamp your foot. That'll be the body falling. Time me from there.

The 8TH JUROR *lies down on the two chairs.*

7TH JUROR: Anyone for charades?

3RD JUROR: I've never seen anything like this in my whole life!

8TH JUROR: OK. I'm ready.

The 2ND JUROR *stares at his watch, waiting.*

10TH JUROR: Come on, let's go here.

2ND JUROR: I want to wait until the second hand reaches sixty. *They wait. The* 2ND JUROR *suddenly stamps his foot. The* 8TH JUROR *rises to a sitting position, swings his legs to the floor and stands up. The* 2ND JUROR *keeps his eyes on his watch. The* 8TH JUROR *hobbles, dragging one leg, toward the chair that serves as the bedroom door. He reaches it and pretends to open the door. He then hobbles along the simulated forty-three-foot hallway.*

10TH JUROR: Come on. Snap it up. He walked twice as fast as that.

11TH JUROR: This is, I think, even more quickly than the old man walked in the courtroom.

8TH JUROR [*still hobbling*]: If you think I should go faster, I will.

The 8TH JUROR *speeds up his pace slightly, reaches the wall, turns and heads for the second chair, the one simulating the door to the outer hallway.*

3RD JUROR: Come on, willya! Let's get this kid stuff over with. *They watch as the* 8TH JUROR *reaches the last chair. He pretends to open an imaginary chain lock and then opens the imaginary door.*

8TH JUROR: Stop!

2ND JUROR: Right.

8TH JUROR: What's the time?

2ND JUROR: Fifteen—twenty—thirty—thirty-five—forty—forty-two seconds exactly.

6TH JUROR: Forty-two seconds!

8TH JUROR: I think this is what happened. The old man heard the fight between the boy and his father a few hours earlier. Then, while lying in bed, he heard a body hit the floor in the boy's apartment, and he heard the woman scream from across the street. He got up, tried to get to the door, heard someone racing down the stairs, and assumed it was the boy.

6TH JUROR: I think that's possible.

3RD JUROR: Assumed? Now listen to me, you people. I've seen all kinds of dishonesty in my day—but this little display takes the cake. You come in here with your sanctimonious talk about slum kids and injustice, and you make up some wild stories, and all of a sudden you start getting through to some of these old ladies in here. Well, you're not getting through to me. I've had enough. What's the matter with you people? Every one of you knows this kid is guilty. He's got to burn. We're letting him slip through our fingers here.

8TH JUROR: Slip through our fingers? Are you his executioner?

3RD JUROR: I'm one of 'em.

8TH JUROR: Maybe you'd like to pull the switch.

3RD JUROR: For this kid? You bet I'd like to pull the switch.

8TH JUROR: I'm sorry for you.

3RD JUROR: Don't start with me now.

8TH JUROR: Ever since we walked into this room you've been behaving like a self-appointed public avenger.

3RD JUROR: I'm telling you now! Shut up!

8TH JUROR: You want to see this boy die because you personally want it, not because of the facts.

3RD JUROR: Shut up!

8TH JUROR: You're a sadist!

3RD JUROR: Shut up, you son of a bitch!

The 3RD JUROR *lunges wildly at the* 8TH JUROR.

The 8TH JUROR *holds his ground. The* 5TH *and* 6TH JURORS *grab the* 3RD JUROR *from behind. He strains against the hands, his face dark with rage.*

Let go of me, God damn it! I'll kill him! I'll kill him!

8TH JUROR [*calmly*]: You don't really mean you'll kill me, do you?

The 3RD JUROR *breaks from the* 5TH *and* 6TH JURORS, *stops struggling and stares bitterly at the* 8TH JUROR *as*

—*the* CURTAIN *falls.*

ACT II

The same. Immediately following.

When the CURTAIN *rises, the* JURORS *are in the same positions as they were at the end of the previous act, looking at the* 3RD JUROR. *There is silence. The* 3RD JUROR *crosses to the window. The other* JURORS *move about the room. There is an awkward silence.*

The GUARD *unlocks the door and enters.*

GUARD: Is there anything wrong, gentlemen? I heard some noise.

FOREMAN: No. There's nothing wrong.
  The FOREMAN *collects the apartment plan from the table.*
  Just a little argument. Everything's OK.
  The FOREMAN *hands the plan to the* GUARD.
  We're finished with this.
  The GUARD *takes the plan, looks carefully around the room, then exits, locking the door behind him.*
  There is a pause. The others look at the 3RD JUROR.

3RD JUROR: Well, what are you staring at?
  The others, embarrassed, turn away. Some of them take their seats.

12TH JUROR: Well—I suppose someone has to—start it off again.

2ND JUROR: It's getting late. [*To the* FOREMAN.] What do they do, take us out to a restaurant for supper?

FOREMAN: How do I know?

2ND JUROR: I wonder if they let us go home in case we can't

finish tonight. I've got a boy with mumps. He's out to here. The wife says he looks like Khrushchev.

The room begins to darken perceptibly now.

11TH JUROR: Pardon. This fighting. This is not why we are here, to fight. We have a responsibility. This, I have always thought, is a remarkable thing about democracy. That we are, uh, what is the word? Notified. That we are notified by mail to come down to this place and decide on the guilt or innocence of a man we have never heard of before. We have nothing to gain or lose by our verdict. This is one of the reasons we are strong. We should not make it a personal thing.

12TH JUROR: Um, if no one else has an idea, I may have a cutie here. I mean, I haven't put much thought into it. Anyway, lemme throw it out on the stoop and see if the cat licks it up.

FOREMAN: See if the cat licks it up? [*He laughs.*]

12TH JUROR: Well, it wasn't much of an idea, anyway.

5TH JUROR: Look how dark it's getting. We're gonna have a storm. Boy, it's hot.

The 4TH JUROR, in tie and jacket, is seemingly not bothered by the heat at all. The 5TH JUROR turns to him.

Pardon me, don't you sweat?

4TH JUROR: No. I don't.

6TH JUROR: Uh, listen, I was wondering if maybe we shouldn't take another vote.

7TH JUROR: Great idea. Maybe we can follow this one up with dancing and refreshments.

6TH JUROR: Mr. Foreman?

FOREMAN: It's all right with me. Anyone doesn't want to vote?

No one answers for a moment.

3RD JUROR: I think we ought to have an open ballot. Call out your votes, y'know. Let's see who stands where.

FOREMAN: That sounds fair. Anyone object? The last vote was eight to four in favor of guilty. All right. I'll call off your jury numbers. I vote "guilty." Number Two?

2ND JUROR: "Not Guilty."

FOREMAN: Number Three?

3RD JUROR: "Guilty."

FOREMAN: Number Four?

4TH JUROR: "Guilty."

FOREMAN: Number Five?

5TH JUROR: "Not Guilty."

FOREMAN: Number Six?

6TH JUROR: "Not Guilty."

FOREMAN: Number Seven?

7TH JUROR: "Guilty."

FOREMAN: Number Eight?

8TH JUROR: "Not Guilty."

FOREMAN: Number Nine?

9TH JUROR: "Not Guilty."

FOREMAN: Number Ten?

1OTH JUROR: "Guilty."

FOREMAN: Number Eleven?

11TH JUROR: "Not Guilty."

FOREMAN: Number Twelve?

12TH JUROR: "Guilty."

FOREMAN: Six to six.

7TH JUROR: And we go into extra innings here.

1OTH JUROR: Six to six! I'm telling you, some of you people in here are out of your minds. A kid like that.

9TH JUROR: I don't think the kind of boy he is has anything to do with it. The facts are supposed to determine the case.

1OTH JUROR: Ah, don't give me any of that. I'm sick and tired of facts. You can twist 'em any way you like. Know what I mean?

9TH JUROR: That's exactly the point this gentleman [*He indicates the* 8TH JUROR.] has been making. I mean, you keep shouting at the top of your lungs . . .

The 8TH JUROR *puts his hand on the* 9TH JUROR's *shoulder. The* 9TH JUROR *looks at him and sits.*

I'd like to be a little younger. [*He stops. Unable to go on.*] It's very hot in here.

11TH JUROR: Do you want some water?

9TH JUROR: No, thanks.

It has grown considerably darker in the room and it's oppressively still. There is a murmur of voices at the cooler where the 7TH, 1OTH, *and* 2ND JURORS *are in various stages of getting a drink.*

2ND JUROR: It's going to rain.

7TH JUROR: No! How did you figure that out, blue eyes? Tell me, how come you switched?

2ND JUROR: Well, it just seemed to me—

7TH JUROR: I mean, you haven't got a leg to stand on. You know that, don'tcha?

2ND JUROR: Well, I don't feel that way. There're a lot of details that never came out.

10TH JUROR: Details! You're just letting yourself get bulldozed by a bunch'a what d'ya call 'em—intellectuals.

2ND JUROR: Now, that's not so.

10TH JUROR: Ah, come on. You're like everybody else. You think too much, you get mixed up. Know what I mean?

2ND JUROR: Now, listen, I don't think you have any right to . . .

The 10TH JUROR *crosses away.*

[*Softly.*] Loudmouth!

It is now darker than before. There is no movement in the room. Everyone waits for the storm. And suddenly it comes. We hear only the sound of the rain pouring down into the silence. Heads turn toward the window. The rain pours down. The 4TH JUROR *goes into the washroom and exits to the lavatory.*

The 8TH JUROR *steps back from the window as the rain splashes in, closes it. The* FOREMAN *rises, goes to the light switch at the door and switches on the lights. There is a flickering of harsh white light as the fluorescent lights come on. The rain continues throughout the remainder of the play. The* FOREMAN *moves to the* 8TH JUROR.

FOREMAN: Wow! Look at that come down, will ya? Think it'll cool things off?

8TH JUROR: Yeah, I guess so.

FOREMAN: Boy! Look at it go! Reminds me of the storm we had—November something. What a storm! Right in the middle of the game.

The 3RD JUROR *crosses to the washroom, goes in, switches on the light and washes his hands.*

We're behind seven-six, but we're just startin' to move the ball, off tackle, y'know. Boom! Boom! Boy, I'll never forget that. We had this kid, Slattery. A real ox. Wish I had another one like him. Oh, I probably forgot to tell you—I'm assistant head football coach at the Andrew J. McCorkle High School. That's in Queens.

The 8TH JUROR *smiles briefly.*

So anyway, we're movin' real nice. Their line is comin' apart. I'm tellin' ya, this Slattery. Boy! And all of a sudden it starts to come down cats and dogs. In two minutes it was mud practically up to your ass. I swear I almost bawled. We couldn't go nowhere.

7TH JUROR: Hey, let's try to get this fan goin' in here. What d'ya say?

The 4TH JUROR *enters the washroom from the lavatory.*

The FOREMAN *goes to the bench, stands on it and starts the fan.*

It musta been connected to the light switch.

The 3RD *and* 4TH JURORS *are in the washroom together.*

3RD JUROR [*to the* 4TH JUROR]: Some rain, huh?

The 4TH JUROR *nods.*

Well, what d'ya think of this thing? It's even-steven.

The 4TH JUROR *nods.*

Kind of surprising, isn't it?

4TH JUROR: Yes.

3RD JUROR: Listen, that business before, you know, where that guy was baiting me. I mean, that doesn't prove anything. Listen, I'm a very excitable person, y'know. So where does he get off to call me a public avenger and a sadist and everything? Anybody in his right mind'd blow his stack, wouldn't he? He was just trying to bait me.

4TH JUROR: He did an excellent job. [*He moves to the towel.*] Excuse me. [*He dries his hands.*]

3RD JUROR: OK, maybe he did. I told you, I can't help that kind of thing. I'm a certain type of person, I get moved by this. But let me tell you, I'm sincere.

4TH JUROR: Fine. We all are.

The 10TH JUROR *bursts into the washroom, strides to the basin and washes his hands.*

10TH JUROR: Well—isn't this the goddamnedest thing you ever saw? Six to six. It's a joke.

3RD JUROR: What are we gonna do about it? Can't we break it somehow?

10TH JUROR: Those six bastards in there aren't going to change their minds.

4TH JUROR: Five of them already have changed their minds. There's no reason why they can't be persuaded to do it again.

10TH JUROR: How?

4TH JUROR: Just by using logic.

10TH JUROR: Logic! Holy cow!

3RD JUROR: Now, just you listen to this man. He's the only one in the room who knows . . .

10TH JUROR: You want my opinion?

4TH JUROR: Go ahead.

10TH JUROR: I think we should just quit.

3RD JUROR: What the hell are you talking about?

10TH JUROR: Those people in there are suddenly like it's some kind of mission or something. Look, they're not gonna switch, so let's go and tell the Judge—we'll be here all night. For Chrissakes, let's tell him we're hung. The hell with this. I mean, what am I gonna do, break my brains over scum like that?

3RD JUROR: Well, that's the most ridiculous thing I ever . . . You took an oath in the courtroom. You can't just quit.

10TH JUROR: Why not?

3RD JUROR: It's dishonest. Why don't you vote "not guilty"?

10TH JUROR: I voted guilty because I think he's guilty.

3RD JUROR: But now you don't care what happens?

10TH JUROR: No. Why should I?

4TH JUROR: All right, let's stop this. We're not going to get anywhere like this.

10TH JUROR: Well, what does he want? I gave my honest opinion.

4TH JUROR: I know.

10TH JUROR: I suppose you don't think much of it?

4TH JUROR: No, I don't.

The FOREMAN *opens the washroom door.*

FOREMAN: Uh—we'd like to get going in here again, if you don't mind.

The 4TH JUROR *leaves the washroom.*

10TH JUROR [*to the* 3RD JUROR]: How about him? Is that something?

3RD JUROR: A hung jury doesn't mean anything. They just have to start the trial with another jury. That's not what we're here for.

10TH JUROR: What the hell's the difference? A hung jury is what you're gonna get.

FOREMAN: Look, would you please . . .

The 10TH JUROR *strides out of the washroom, the* 3RD JUROR *switches out the light and comes slowly into the room.*

10TH JUROR: Listen, I'll tell you what I think. We're goin' nowhere here. I'm ready to walk into court right now and declare a hung jury.

7TH JUROR: I go for that, too. Let's take it into the Judge and let the kid take his chances with twelve other guys.

8TH JUROR: I don't think the court will accept a hung jury. We haven't been in here very long.

7TH JUROR: Well, let's find out.

11TH JUROR: I'm not in favor of this.

7TH JUROR [*to the* 11TH JUROR]: Listen, this kid wouldn't stand a chance with another jury and you know it. [*To the others.*] Come on, we're hung. Nobody's gonna change his opinion. Let's take it inside.

5TH JUROR: You still don't think there's any room for reasonable doubt?

7TH JUROR: No, I don't.

11TH JUROR: Pardon. Maybe you don't fully understand the term "reasonable doubt."

7TH JUROR: What d'ya mean, I don't understand it? Who the hell are you to talk to me like that? [*To the others.*] How d'ya like this guy? I'm tellin' ya they're all alike. He comes over to this country running for his life and before he can even take a big breath he's telling us how to run the show. The arrogance of the guy!

5TH JUROR [*to the* 7TH JUROR]: You mean you're calling him arrogant because he wasn't born here? Well, I'm calling you arrogant because you were. How's that?

11TH JUROR: Please, please. It doesn't matter.

7TH JUROR: Look, sonny, nobody around here's gonna tell me what words I understand and what words I don't. [*He points to the* 11TH JUROR.] Especially him. Because I'll knock his goddamn Middle European head off.

FOREMAN: All right. Let's stop arguing for two minutes in here. Can't we stick to the subject?

8TH JUROR: I'd like to go over something, if you gentlemen don't mind. An important point for the prosecution was the fact that the boy, after he claimed he was at the movies during the hours the killing took place, couldn't name the pictures he saw or the stars who appeared in them. [*He points to the* 4TH JUROR.] This gentleman has repeated that point in here several times.

4TH JUROR: That's correct. It was the only alibi the boy offered and he himself couldn't back it up with any details at all.

8TH JUROR: Putting yourself in the boy's place, if you can, do you think you'd be able to remember details after an upsetting experience such as being struck in the face by your father?

4TH JUROR: I think so, if there were any special details to remember. He couldn't remember the movies at the theater he named because he wasn't there that night.

8TH JUROR: According to the police testimony in court he was questioned by the police in the kitchen of his apartment while the body of his father was lying on the floor in the bedroom. Do you think you could remember details under such circumstances?

4TH JUROR: I do.

8TH JUROR: Under great emotional stress?

4TH JUROR: Under great emotional stress.

8TH JUROR: He remembered the movies in court. He named them correctly and he named the stars who played in them.

4TH JUROR: Yes, his lawyer took great pains to bring that out. He had three months from the night of the murder to the day of the trial in which to memorize them. I'll take the testimony of the policeman who interrogated him right after the murder, when he couldn't remember a thing about the movies, great emotional stress or not.

8TH JUROR: I'd like to ask you a personal question.

4TH JUROR: Go ahead.

8TH JUROR: Where were you last night?

4TH JUROR: I was home.

8TH JUROR: What about the night before last?

10TH JUROR: Come on, what is this?

4TH JUROR [*to the* 10TH JUROR]: It's perfectly all right. [*To the* 8TH JUROR.] I went from court to my office and stayed there till eight thirty. Then I went straight home to bed.

8TH JUROR: And the night before that?

4TH JUROR: That was—Tuesday. I—was—oh, yes. That was the night of the bridge tournament. I played bridge.

8TH JUROR: And Monday night.

7TH JUROR: When you get him down to New Year's Eve, nineteen fifty lemme know.

4TH JUROR [*trying to remember*]: Monday. [*He pauses.*] Monday night. [*He remembers.*] Monday night my wife and I went to the movies.

8TH JUROR: What did you see?

4TH JUROR: *The Scarlet Circle.* It's a very clever whodunit.

8TH JUROR: What was the second feature?

4TH JUROR [*straining*]: The . . . I'll tell you in a minute. *The— Remarkable Mrs. Something.* Mrs.—uh—Mainbridge. No, Bainbridge. *The Remarkable Mrs. Bainbridge.*

2ND JUROR: Excuse me. I saw that. It's called *The Amazing Mrs. Bainbridge.*

4TH JUROR: *The—Amazing Mrs. Bainbridge.* Yes. I think that's right.

8TH JUROR: Who was in *The Amazing Mrs. Bainbridge*?

4TH JUROR: Barbara—Long, I think. She's a dark, very pretty girl. Barbara—Lang—Lane—something like that.

8TH JUROR: Who else?

The 4TH JUROR *takes a handkerchief and mops his suddenly sweating forehead.*

4TH JUROR: Well, I'd never heard of them before. It was a very inexpensive second feature, with unknown . . .

8TH JUROR: And you weren't under an emotional strain, were you?

4TH JUROR: No, I wasn't.

9TH JUROR: I think the point is made.

10TH JUROR: Big point!

9TH JUROR: I think it is a big point.

10TH JUROR: What? Just because he can't remember the name of some two-bit movie star? I suppose that proves the kid was at the movies.

9TH JUROR: No. But it indicates that no one can prove he wasn't. He might have been at the movies and forgotten what he saw. It's possible. If it's perfectly normal for this gentleman [*he indicates the* 4TH JUROR]—to forget a few details, then it's also perfectly normal for the boy. Being accused of murder isn't necessarily supposed to give him an infallible memory.

10TH JUROR [*to the* 9TH JUROR]: You can talk till your tongue is draggin' on the floor. The boy is guilty. Period. Know what I mean, my friend? Who's got those cough drops?

2ND JUROR: They're all gone, my friend.

FOREMAN: Y'know, there's something we're forgetting here that I was just thinking about. That whole business with the psychiatrist that dragged on forever.

10TH JUROR: Now don't start with all that phoney psycho-whatever-you-call-it-stuff. What a racket that is! Filling people's heads with all that junk. Listen, I've got three psychiatrists keeping their cars in one of my garages. The whole three of 'em are crazy.

FOREMAN: Listen, there's a point I'm tryin' to make here. Do you mind?

10TH JUROR: I wouldn't give you a nickel for a psychiatrist's testimony.

8TH JUROR: Why don't you let the man talk? You can take five minutes on the uselessness of psychiatry when he's finished.

FOREMAN: What I was gonna say was, the psychiatrist definitely stated that the boy had strong homicidal tendencies. I mean, that he was, what d'ya call it—capable of committing murder. He described all those tests, inkblots and all that stuff, and he said the kid is definitely a killer type. Am I right?

12TH JUROR: Check. I think he said something about paranoid tendencies if I'm not mistaken.

FOREMAN: Right. Whatever that is, he said it. Let's not forget, we're talking about a boy who always had murder on his mind.

12TH JUROR: His unconscious mind.

FOREMAN: Nobody else's.

11TH JUROR: I beg pardon, in discussing—

10TH JUROR: I beg pardon. What are you so goddamn polite about?

11TH JUROR: For the same reason you're not. It's the way I was brought up. [*He turns to the others.*] In discussing such a thing as the murder potential we should remember that many of us are capable of committing murder. But few of us do. We impose controls upon ourselves to prevent it. The most these psychiatric tests can accomplish along these lines is this: they can tell us that someday a particular person may commit a murder. That's all. They prove nothing.

4TH JUROR: Then how come they're admitted in evidence?

11TH JUROR: They have many uses, of course. In this case they added to the general impression the prosecution was trying to create. Perhaps we would find that if we twelve men took the same tests, one or two of us might be discovered to have unconscious desires to kill, and the potentiality of carrying them out. Yet none of us has. To say that a man is capable of murder does not mean that he has committed murder.

10TH JUROR: But it can mean it. Listen, if they said the kid is capable of killing, he could've killed, couldn't he?

8TH JUROR: You're the one who said, and I quote, "I wouldn't give you a nickel for a psychiatrist's testimony."

10TH JUROR: Boy, I'm telling you . . . [*He crosses to the* 8TH JUROR.] I'd like to . . . [*He stops.*]

The 8TH JUROR *does not look up at him. The* 10TH JUROR *crosses angrily away.*

6TH JUROR: What time is it?

7TH JUROR: It's five of six. Man, look at that rain.

12TH JUROR: There goes your ball game.

2ND JUROR [*to the* 8TH JUROR]: Say, could I see that knife for a second?

The 8TH JUROR *slides the knife across the table to the* 2ND JUROR, *who opens and examines it.*

FOREMAN: Well, we're still tied up six to six. Who's got a suggestion?

12TH JUROR: I have. Let's get some dinner.

5TH JUROR: Why don't we wait till seven? Give it another hour.

12TH JUROR: OK with me.

2ND JUROR: Um—there's something I'd like to say. I mean, it's been bothering me a little and as long as we're stuck. . . . Well, there was this whole business about the stab wound and how it was made, the downward angle of it, you know?

3RD JUROR: Don't tell me we're gonna start with that. They went over it and over it.

2ND JUROR: I know they did, but I don't go along with it. The boy is five feet, seven inches tall. His father was six two. That's a difference of seven inches. It's a very awkward thing to stab down into the chest of someone who's more than a half a foot taller than you are.

3RD JUROR [crossing to the 2ND JUROR and indicating the knife]: Give me that.

The 2ND JUROR hands the knife to the 3RD JUROR.

Look, you're not gonna be satisfied till you see it again. I'm gonna give you a demonstration. Somebody get up.

There is a pause. No one moves for a moment, and then the 8TH JUROR rises and crosses to the 3RD JUROR. They stand looking at each other.

OK. [To the 2ND JUROR.] Now, watch this. I don't want to have to do it again. [He turns to the 8TH JUROR, looks squarely at him, and squats to make himself shorter.] I'm six or seven inches shorter than you. Right?

2ND JUROR: That's right. Maybe a little more.

3RD JUROR: OK. Let it be more.

The 3RD JUROR flicks open the knife, changes its position in his hand and holds it aloft, ready to stab downwards.

The 8TH JUROR and the 3RD JUROR look steadily at each other, then the 3RD JUROR suddenly stabs downward, hard.

2ND JUROR: Look out!

The blade stops about an inch from the 8TH JUROR's chest. The 8TH JUROR does not move. The 3RD JUROR smiles.

6TH JUROR: That's not funny.

5TH JUROR: What's the matter with you?

3RD JUROR: Now just calm down. Nobody's hurt. Right?

8TH JUROR: No. Nobody's hurt.

3RD JUROR: All right. There's your angle. Take a look at it. Down and in. That's how I'd stab a taller man in the chest and that's how it was done. Now go ahead and tell me I'm wrong. *The* 3RD JUROR *hands the knife to the* 8TH JUROR *and crosses away. The* 12TH JUROR *crosses to the* 8TH JUROR *and using his closed hand, simulates stabbing the* 8TH JUROR *in the chest.*

12TH JUROR: Down and in. I guess there's no argument.

5TH JUROR [*moving to the* 8TH JUROR]: Wait a minute. Give me that. *The* 8TH JUROR *hands the knife to the* 5TH JUROR. *He closes the knife and holds it gingerly.* I hate these things. I grew up with them.

8TH JUROR: Have you seen them used in fights?

5TH JUROR: Too many of them. On my stoop. In my backyard. In the lot across the street. Switch knives came with the neighborhood where I lived. Funny, I wasn't thinking of it. I guess you try to forget those things. You don't use this kind of knife that way. You have to hold it like this to release the blade. In order to stab downward, you would have to change your grip.

8TH JUROR: How do you use it?

5TH JUROR: Underhanded. *The* 5TH JUROR *flicks the knife open and, holding it underhanded, swings round and slashes swiftly forward and upward.* Like that. Anyone who's ever used a switch knife'd never handle it any other way.

8TH JUROR: Are you sure?

5TH JUROR: I'm sure. *The* 5TH JUROR *closes the blade and flicks it open again.* That's why they're made like this.

8TH JUROR: Everyone agreed that the boy is pretty handy with a knife, didn't they?

5TH JUROR: That's right.

8TH JUROR [to the 5TH JUROR]: Do you think he would have made the kind of wound that killed his father?

5TH JUROR: Not with the experience he'd had with these things. No, I don't think he would. He'd go for him underhanded . . .

3RD JUROR: How do you know? What—were you in the room when the father was killed?

5TH JUROR: No, and neither was anyone else.

The 5TH JUROR sticks the knife in the table and crosses away.

3RD JUROR [to the 8TH JUROR]: You're giving us a lot of mumbo-jumbo here. I don't believe it.

4TH JUROR: I don't think you can determine what type of wound this boy might or might not have made simply because he knows how to handle a knife.

3RD JUROR: That's right. That's absolutely right.

8TH JUROR [looking at the 12TH JUROR]: What do you think?

The 12TH JUROR hesitates for a moment. He is confused, but trying to be honest.

12TH JUROR: Well—I don't know . . .

3RD JUROR: What d'ya mean—you don't know?

12TH JUROR: I don't know.

8TH JUROR [to the 7TH JUROR]: What about you?

The 7TH JUROR looks around the table momentarily.

4TH JUROR: Just a minute. According to the woman across the street . . .

7TH JUROR: Listen, I'll tell you something. I'm a little sick of this whole thing already. All this yakkin's gettin' us nowhere so I'm going to break it up here. I'm changing my vote to "not guilty."

3RD JUROR: You're what?

7TH JUROR: You heard me. I've had enough.

3RD JUROR: What d'you mean—you've had enough? That's no answer.

7TH JUROR: Hey, listen you! Just worry about yourself!

11TH JUROR [crossing to the 7TH JUROR]: He's right. That is not an answer. What kind of man are you? You have sat here and voted guilty with everyone else because there are some baseball tickets burning a hole in your pocket. Now you have

changed your vote because you say you're sick of all the talking here.

7TH JUROR: Listen. buddy—

11TH JUROR: You have no right to play like this with a man's
life. This is a terrible and ugly thing to do. Don't you care . . . ?

7TH JUROR: Now, wait a minute. You can't talk like that to me!

11TH JUROR: I can talk like that to you. If you want to vote
not guilty, then do it because you're convinced the man is not
guilty—not because you've had enough. And if you think he's
guilty, then vote that way, or don't you have the guts to do
what you think is right?

7TH JUROR: Now, listen . . .

11TH JUROR: Guilty or not guilty?

7TH JUROR: I told you—not guilty.

11TH JUROR: Why?

7TH JUROR: Goddamn you. I don't have to—

11TH JUROR: You do have to. Say it. Why?

7TH JUROR [*in a low voice*]: I—don't think he's guilty.

The 11TH JUROR *looks disgustedly at the* 7TH JUROR, *then
moves to his chair. The* 7TH JUROR *stands defeated.*

8TH JUROR: Mr. Foreman, I want another vote.

FOREMAN: OK, there's another vote called for.

The JURORS *cross to their chairs and sit.*

I guess the quickest way is a show of hands. Anybody object?
There is no answer.

All those voting "not guilty" raise your hands.

The 2ND, 5TH, 6TH, 7TH, 8TH, 9TH, *and* 11TH JURORS *raise
their hands immediately.*

One. Two. Three. Four. Five. Six. Seven.

The 12TH JUROR's *face is a mask of indecision, then he suddenly raises his hand.*

Eight.

The FOREMAN *stops counting and looks around the table.
Slowly, almost embarrassed, he raises his own hand.*

Nine. [*He lowers his hand.*] All those voting "guilty."

The 3RD, 4TH, *and* 10TH JURORS *raise their hands.*

Nine to three in favor of "not guilty."

10TH JUROR: I don't understand you people. I mean, all these

picky little points you keep bringing up. They don't mean nothing. How can you believe his story? [*To the* 11TH JUROR.]
You're an intelligent man. Well, you're not gonna tell me you're
not. You know the facts of life. Well, for Chrissakes look at
what we're dealing with here. You know what they're like! I
mean, that guy [*he points to the* 8TH JUROR]—over there, well,
I don't know what the hell is going on with him. All that talk
about psychiatrists. Maybe he oughta go to one. Look, let's talk
facts. These people are born to lie. Now, it's the way they are
and no intelligent man is gonna tell me otherwise. They don't
know what the truth is. Well, take a look at them. They are different. They think different. They act different. Well, for in-
stance, they don't need any big excuse to kill someone.
The 5TH JUROR *crosses to the washroom door.*
Well, that's true. Everybody knows it. They get drunk on wine
or something cheap like that. Oh, they're very big drinkers.
The 5TH JUROR *goes into the washroom, slams the door behind him.*
Smart guy! Look at him for Chrissakes! What does that
mean, slamming the door? And then they're drunk, and all of
a sudden—bang—somebody's lying dead in the gutter. OK,
nobody's blaming them for it. That's how they are, by nature, y'know what I mean? Violent! Human life don't mean
as much to them as it does to us.
The 11TH JUROR *rises and crosses to the washroom door. He
follows the* 5TH JUROR.
Where are you going?
The 11TH JUROR *does not reply and goes into the washroom.*
While you're in there, clean out your ears, maybe you'll hear
something.
The 4TH JUROR *rises and moves to the window.*
Look, you listen to me now. These people are boozing it up,
and fighting all the time, and if somebody gets killed, so
somebody gets killed. They don't care. Family don't mean
anything to them. They breed like animals. Fathers, mothers,
that don't mean anything. Oh sure, there are some good
things about 'em. Look, I'm the first one to say that. I've
known some who were OK, but that's the exception.

9TH JUROR: Do you know you're a sick man?

10TH JUROR: Sick?

9TH JUROR: Why don't you sit down?

10TH JUROR: You old son of a bitch! Who the hell are you?
The 6TH JUROR *moves toward the* 9TH JUROR.
The 12TH JUROR *steps between the* 9TH *and* 10TH JURORS.
[*To the* 12TH JUROR.] No. Who the hell is he to tell me that?
Sick. Look at him—he can hardly stand up. Listen, I'm
speaking my piece here and you're gonna listen.
The 9TH JUROR *moves to the window.*

12TH JUROR: Maybe if you just quieted down.

10TH JUROR: I will like hell quiet down. There is not one of
them, not one who's any good. Now, d'you hear that? Not
one. Now let me lay this out for you—ignorant—bastards. [*To
the* 9TH JUROR.] You at the window, you're so goddamned
smart. We're facing a danger here. Don't you know it? These
people are multiplying. That kid on trial, his type, they're multiplying five times as fast as we are. That's the statistic. Five
times. And they are—wild animals. They're against us, they
hate us, they want to destroy us. That's right. [*To the* 6TH JU-
ROR.] Don't look at me like that! There's a danger. For God's
sake, we're living in a dangerous time, and if we don't watch
it, if we don't smack them down whenever we can, then they
are gonna own us. They're gonna breed us out of existence.

6TH JUROR: Ah, shut up!

10TH JUROR: Now you goddamned geniuses had better listen
to me. They're violent, they're vicious, they're ignorant, and
they will cut us up. That's their intent. To cut us up. [*To the*
7TH JUROR.] I'm warning you. This boy, this boy on trial
here. We've got him. That's one at least. I say get him before
his kind gets us. I don't give a goddamn about the law. Why
should I? They don't. Now I'm telling you.

2ND JUROR: I've heard enough. Now you just stop all this.

10TH JUROR [*looking angrily at the* 2ND JUROR]: How would
you like me to cave your head in for you, you smart little bas-
tard? Where the hell do you get the gall . . . ?
The 4TH JUROR *steps in front of the* 10TH JUROR *and stops
him firmly.*

4TH JUROR: We've heard enough. Sit down. And don't open your filthy mouth again.

The 4TH *and* 10TH JURORS *stare at each other. Finally, the* 10TH JUROR *turns away, crosses to a chair and sits with his back to the others. The other* JURORS [*including the* 5TH *and* 11TH JURORS] *slowly cross to their seats.*

8TH JUROR: It's very hard to keep personal prejudice out of a thing like this. And no matter where you run into it, prejudice obscures the truth. Well, I don't think any real damage has been done here. Because I don't really know what the truth is. No one ever will, I suppose. Nine of us now seem to feel that the defendant is innocent, but we're just gambling on probabilities. We may be wrong. We may be trying to return a guilty man to the community. No one can really know. But we have a reasonable doubt, and this is a safeguard that has enormous value in our system. No jury can declare a man guilty unless it's sure. We nine can't understand how you three are still so sure. Maybe you can tell us.

4TH JUROR: I'll try. You've made some excellent points. The last one, in which you argued that the boy wouldn't have made the kind of overhand stab wound that killed his father, was very persuasive. But I still believe the boy is guilty of murder. I have two reasons. One: the evidence given by the woman across the street who actually saw the murder committed.

3RD JUROR: And how, brother! As far as I'm concerned that's the most important testimony in the whole case.

4TH JUROR: And two: the fact that this woman described the stabbing by saying she saw the boy raise his arm over his head and plunge the knife down into his father's chest. She saw him do it—the wrong way.

3RD JUROR: That's right! That's absolutely right!

4TH JUROR: Now, let's talk about this woman for a minute. She said that she went to bed at about eleven o'clock that night. Her bed was next to the window—and she could look out while lying down and see directly into the boy's window across the tracks. She tossed and turned for over an hour, unable to fall asleep. Finally, she turned toward the window at about ten minutes after twelve, and, as she looked out, she saw the killing through the windows of the passing el train. She says that the lights went out immediately after the killing but that she got a good look at the boy in the act of stabbing his father. As far as I can see, this is unshakeable testimony.

3RD JUROR: That's what I mean. That's the whole case.

4TH JUROR [*to the* 8TH JUROR]: What do you think?

The 8TH JUROR *remains silent.*

[*Looking at the* 12TH JUROR.] How about you?

12TH JUROR: Well—I don't know. There's so much evidence to sift. This is a pretty complicated business.

4TH JUROR: Frankly, I don't see how we can vote for acquittal.

12TH JUROR: Well, it's not so easy to arrange the evidence in order.

3RD JUROR: You can throw out all the other evidence. The woman saw him do it. What else do you want?

12TH JUROR: Well, maybe . . .

3RD JUROR: Let's vote on it.

FOREMAN: OK. There's another vote called for. Anybody object?

12TH JUROR: I'm changing my vote. I think he's "guilty."

3RD JUROR: Anybody else? The vote is eight to four.

11TH JUROR [*to the* 3RD JUROR]: What makes you consider this one vote a personal triumph?

3RD JUROR: I'm the competitive type. [*To the others.*] OK. Now here's what I think. I think we're a hung jury. Let's take it inside to the Judge.

4TH JUROR: You didn't want a hung jury before.

3RD JUROR: Well, I want it now.

4TH JUROR: I don't understand that. You thought it was immoral to—

3RD JUROR: I don't anymore. There are people in here who are so goddamned stubborn that you can't even . . . We'll never get this thing done. We'll be here for a week. Well, I want to hear an argument. I say we're a hung jury.

[*He turns to the* 8TH JUROR.] Come on. You're the leader of the cause. What about it?

8TH JUROR: Let's go over it again.

3RD JUROR: We went over it again. [*He waves toward the* 12TH

JUROR.] J. Walter Thompson over there is bouncing backward and forward like a tennis ball . . .

12TH JUROR: Wait a second. You have no right to . . .

The 4TH JUROR *removes his spectacles and polishes them.*

3RD JUROR: I apologize on my knees. [*To the* 8TH JUROR.] Come on. Let's get out from under this thing.

4TH JUROR: All right. Maybe we can talk about setting some kind of a time limit. [*Still polishing his spectacles, he turns and peers up at the clock.*] The time is . . . [*He squints and puts on his spectacles.*]

3RD JUROR: Quarter after six.

4TH JUROR [*looking at the clock*]: Quarter after six. [*He removes his spectacles and lays them on the table. He looks tired. He closes his eyes and clasps his fingers over the marks left by his spectacles at the sides of his nose. He rubs these areas as he speaks.*] Someone before mentioned seven o'clock. I think that's a point at which we might begin to discuss the question of whether we're a hung jury or not.

The 9TH JUROR *looks closely at the* 4TH JUROR *and obviously has thought of something tremendously exciting.*

9TH JUROR [*to the* 4TH JUROR]: Don't you feel well?

4TH JUROR: I feel perfectly well—thank you. [*To the others.*] I was saying that seven o'clock would be a reasonable time to—

9TH JUROR: The reason I asked about that was because you were rubbing your nose like . . . I'm sorry for interrupting. But you made a gesture that reminded me—

4TH JUROR: I'm trying to settle something here. Do you mind?

9TH JUROR: I think this is important.

4TH JUROR: Very well.

9TH JUROR: Thank you. I'm sure you'll pardon me for this, but I was wondering why you were rubbing your nose like that?

3RD JUROR: Ah, come on, now, will ya please!

9TH JUROR: Right now I happen to be talking to this gentleman here. [*To the* 4TH JUROR.] Now, why were you rubbing your nose?

4TH JUROR: Well, if it's any of your business, I was rubbing it because it bothers me a little.

9TH JUROR: I'm sorry. Is it because of your eyeglasses?

4TH JUROR: It is. Now could we get on to something else?

9TH JUROR: Your eyeglasses make those deep impressions on the sides of your nose. I hadn't noticed that before. They must be annoying.

4TH JUROR: They are very annoying.

9TH JUROR: I wouldn't know about that. I've never worn eyeglasses. [*He points to his eyes and smiles.*] Twenty-twenty.

7TH JUROR: Listen, will you come on already with the optometrist bit.

9TH JUROR [*to the* 4TH JUROR]: The woman who testified that she saw the killing had these same deep marks on the sides of her nose.

8TH JUROR: That's right, she did.

There is a silence in the room and then a babble of ad lib conversation.

9TH JUROR: Please. Just a minute and then I'll be finished. I don't know if anyone else noticed that about her. I didn't think about it then, but I've been going over her face in my mind. She had those marks. She kept rubbing them in court.

5TH JUROR: He's right. She did do that a lot.

9TH JUROR: This woman was about forty-five years old. She was making a tremendous effort to look thirty-five for her first public appearance. Heavy make-up. Dyed hair. Brand-new clothes that should have been worn by a younger woman. No eyeglasses. See if you can get a mental picture of her.

3RD JUROR: What d'ya mean, no glasses? You don't know if she wore glasses. Just because she was rubbing her nose . . .

5TH JUROR: She has those marks. I saw 'em.

3RD JUROR: So what? What d'ya think that means?

FOREMAN: Listen, I saw 'em, too. He's right. I was the closest one to her. She had these deep things, what d'ya call 'em, uh— you know.

The FOREMAN *massages the spot on his nose where they should be.*

3RD JUROR: Well, what point are you making here?

FOREMAN: She had those marks.

3RD JUROR: She had dyed hair and marks on her nose. I'm asking ya what does that mean?

9TH JUROR: Could those marks be made by anything other than eyeglasses?

4TH JUROR: No. They couldn't.

3RD JUROR [to the 4TH JUROR]: Listen, what are you saying here? I didn't see any marks.

4TH JUROR: I did. Strange, but I didn't think about it before.

3RD JUROR: Well, what about the lawyer? Why didn't he say anything?

8TH JUROR: There are twelve people in here concentrating on this case. Eleven of us didn't think of it, either.

3RD JUROR: OK, Clarence Darrow. Then what about the District Attorney? You think he'd try to pull a trick like that, have her testify without glasses?

8TH JUROR: Did you ever see a woman who had to wear glasses and didn't want to because she thinks they spoil her looks?

6TH JUROR: My wife. Listen, I'm telling ya, as soon as we walk outa the house . . .

8TH JUROR: Maybe the District Attorney didn't know, either.

6TH JUROR: Yeah, that's what I was just gonna say.

3RD JUROR: OK. She had marks on her nose. I'm givin' ya this. From glasses. Right? She never wore 'em out of the house so people'd think she was gorgeous. But when she saw this kid kill his father she was in the house. Alone. That's all.

8TH JUROR [to the 4TH JUROR]: Do you wear your eyeglasses when you go to bed?

4TH JUROR: No, I don't. No one wears eyeglasses to bed.

8TH JUROR: It's logical to say that she wasn't wearing them while she was in bed, tossing and turning, trying to fall asleep.

3RD JUROR: How do you know?

8TH JUROR: I don't know. I'm guessing. I'm also guessing that she probably didn't put on her glasses when she turned and looked casually out of the window. And she herself said that the murder took place just as she looked out and the lights went off a split second later. She couldn't have had time to put glasses on then.

3RD JUROR: Wait a second . . .

8TH JUROR: And here's another guess. Maybe she honestly thought she saw the boy kill his father. I say that she saw only a blur.

3RD JUROR: How do you know what she saw? How does he know all these things? [*To the* 8TH JUROR.] You don't know what kind of glasses she wore. Maybe she was farsighted. Maybe they were sunglasses. What do you know about it?

8TH JUROR: I only know that the woman's eyesight is in question now.

11TH JUROR: She had to identify a person sixty feet away in the dark, without glasses.

2ND JUROR: You can't send someone off to die on evidence like that.

3RD JUROR: Don't give me that!

8TH JUROR: Don't you think that the woman might have made a mistake?

3RD JUROR: No!

8TH JUROR: It's not possible?

3RD JUROR: No! It's not possible.

8TH JUROR [*to the* 12TH JUROR]: Is it possible?

12TH JUROR: Yes. I say "not guilty."

8TH JUROR [*to the* 10TH JUROR]: Do you still think he's guilty?

10TH JUROR: Yes, I think he's guilty. But I couldn't care less. You smart bastards do whatever you want to do.

8TH JUROR: How do you vote?

10TH JUROR: "Not guilty." Do whatever you want.

3RD JUROR: You're the worst son of a . . . I think he's guilty.

8TH JUROR: Does anyone else think he's guilty?

4TH JUROR: No, I'm convinced.

3RD JUROR: What's the matter with you?

4TH JUROR: I now have a reasonable doubt.

9TH JUROR: It's eleven to one.

3RD JUROR: Well, what about all the other evidence? What about all that stuff—the knife—the whole business?

2ND JUROR: You said we could throw out all the other evidence.

8TH JUROR [*to the* 3RD JUROR]: You're alone.

3RD JUROR: I don't care whether I'm alone or not. It's my right.

8TH JUROR: It's your right.

3RD JUROR: Well, what d'ya want? I say he's guilty.

8TH JUROR: We want your arguments.

3RD JUROR: I gave you my arguments.

8TH JUROR: We're not convinced. We want to hear them again. We have as much time as it takes.

3RD JUROR: Everything—every single thing that came out in that courtroom, but I mean everything, says he's guilty. Do you think I'm an idiot or something? You lousy bunch of bleeding hearts. You're not goin' to intimidate me. I'm entitled to my opinion. I can sit in this goddamn room for a year. Somebody say something.

The others watch silently.

Why don'tcha take that stuff about the old man—the old man who lived there—and heard everything. Or take the knife, what—just because he—found one like it? The old man saw him. Right there on the stairs. What's the difference how many seconds it took? What's the difference? Every single thing. The knife falling through a hole in his pocket—you can't prove that he didn't get to the door. Sure you can hobble around the room all you want, but you can't prove it. I'm telling you every single thing that went on has been twisted and turned in here. That business with the glasses, how do you know she didn't have them on? The woman testified in court. Well, what d'ya want? That's it.

The others are silent.

That's the whole case.

The others are silent.

That whole thing about hearing the boy yell? The phrase was "I'm gonna kill you." That's what he said. To his own father. I don't care what kind of man that was. It was his father. That goddamn rotten kid. I know him. What they're like. What they do to you. How they kill you every day. My God, don't you see? How come I'm the only one who sees? Jeez, I can feel that knife goin' in.

8TH JUROR: It's not your boy. He's somebody else.

4TH JUROR: Let him live.

There's a long pause.

3RD JUROR: All right. "Not guilty."

The FOREMAN *moves to the door and knocks on it.*
The GUARD *unlocks the door and enters.*
FOREMAN: We have a verdict.
GUARD: All right, gentlemen. Take your seats in the jury box.
The GUARD *exits.*
The FOREMAN *and the other* JURORS *collect their jackets, etc., and all except the* 3RD *and the* 8TH JURORS *follow him off.*
The 3RD JUROR *remains seated. Finally only he and the* 8TH JUROR *remain in the room. The* 8TH JUROR *puts on his own jacket and brings the* 3RD JUROR's *jacket to him. The* 3RD JUROR *rises. The* 8TH JUROR *helps him on with his jacket.*
The 3RD JUROR *exits.*
The 8TH JUROR *follows, but pauses at the door and looks back at the empty jury room. The knife still sticks into the table. The* 8TH JUROR *exits. The rain has stopped.*

CURTAIN

Furniture and
Property List

On stage: Door with practical lock
Table. *On it:* pencils, notepads, ashtrays
Twelve chairs
Extra chairs (one by the window)
Small table
Watercooler with paper cups. *Over it:* clock
Bench. *Over it:* electric fan (practical)
Wastebasket
Coat hooks. *Over them:* shelf
Windows. *To open* Act I: windows closed. *To open*
Act II: windows open
In washroom: washbasin, soap container, towels

Off stage: Clipboard with list and pen, door key [**Guard**]
Switch knife with tag [**Guard**]
Plan of apartment [**Guard**]

Personal: **Foreman:** watch
2nd Juror: watch, package of cough drops
3rd Juror: notes
4th Juror: newspaper, eyeglasses, tie, handkerchief
7th Juror: watch, chewing gum, handkerchief
8th Juror: switch knife
10th Juror: handkerchief

Lighting Plot

Practical fittings required: fluorescent lighting in jury room with light switch by the door

Act I

To open: Effect of sunlight. Washroom light on

Cue 1   **8th Juror** switches off the washroom light   (Page 30)
            Snap off washroom light

Act II

To open: Lights as at end of previous Act

Cue 2   **2nd Juror**: ". . . looks like Khrushchev."   (Page 50)
            Commence slow dim of general lighting
            for effect of gathering storm

Cue 3   **Foreman** switches on the lights   (Page 52)
            Snap on practical with fluorescent
            flicker effect

Cue 4   **3rd Juror** switches on the washroom light   (Page 52)
            Snap on washroom lighting

Cue 5   **3rd Juror** switches off the washroom light   (Page 55)
            Snap off washroom lighting

Effects Plot